Social defence

Social defence

by

Jørgen Johansen and Brian Martin

IRENE PUBLISHING

Social defence
by Jørgen Johansen and Brian Martin

First published 2019 by Irene Publishing
www.irenepublishing.com

For all kinds of contact with the publisher: irene.publishing@gmail.com

ISBN 978-91-88061-37-9

Layout: J. Johansen

Here you can find links to much of the material we have cited in the book:
www.bmartin.cc/pubs/19sd/

Contents

Acknowledgements

We've each been involved with social defence since the 1980s and learned an enormous amount from those who campaigned with us. We've also benefited from engaging with sceptics, who have provided a necessary spur to keep improving our understanding and arguments.

Brian coordinates a writing group that meets weekly in Wollongong, and showed drafts of passages from the book to others in the group. Useful textual suggestions were provided by Tonya Agostini, Anu Bissoonauth-Bedford, Michelle Eady, Kathy Flynn, Mark Fraser, Xiaoping Gao, Anneleis Humphries, Qiuping Lu, Anne Melano, Renee Middlemost, Ben Morris, Anco Peeters, Leimin Shi, Clara Staples, Zhuoling Tian, Jody Watts and Qinqing Xu.

Jørgen has presented drafts of chapters to participants in the Nordic Nonviolence Studygroup (NORNONS). Majken Jul Sørensen, Stellan Vinthagen, Asma Khalifa, Anton Törnberg, Henrik Frykberg, Bjørn Ihler and Daniel Ritter gave valuable comments. Discussions with students in Peace Studies programs around the world as well as with officers at War Academies in Norway, Turkey and UK have helped to develop a deeper understanding of the strengths and weaknesses of the ideas for a social defence concept.

We sent drafts of the book to quite a few readers and received many valuable suggestions. Thanks to Simon Davies, Jan de Voogd, Antonino Drago, Gene Keyes, Barbara Müller, David Purnell and Lineke Schakenbos, and especially to Marty Branagan, Karen Kennedy and Christine Schweitzer for their extensive comments.

Prologue: a possible future

Few realised what was going to happen before dawn next morning. The tense situation with politicians tweeting with only capital letters had gone on for some weeks, but few thought they would move from rhetoric to action. Prices on imported goods had skyrocketed as the so-called "trade war" escalated, and on social media all sorts of rumours circulated. It was years since anyone could navigate through what was published on social media; much was just plain wrong, other parts sophisticated propaganda, and a lot was political views of all sorts.

When the first drones were observed over many city centres and the Internet was unusually slow, it was obvious for most that an attack was in progress. Many of the local social defence groups met to discuss which of the prepared plans should be activated. The decentralised structure guaranteed that a number of activities were started even if some groups could not meet. As agreed, they had a list of activities that all groups would engage in and in addition another set of plans adapted to the local context aiming for activities in their neighbourhood or their sector of society.

Priority one was communication! It was crucial to inform each other about what they knew for sure about present events and which plans they had activated. To reduce the risk of interference in their lines of communication

they had trained for several parallel ways of informing each other. Most local groups had pigeons ready that would fly to a number of the other social defence groups. Each pigeon would carry a tiny memory card with 10 Gb of encrypted text with information on what each group knew and what they had done to resist a takeover by the foreign power. To avoid surveillance the text on these cards was written on computers that had never been connected to the grid and the receiver read them on similar machines.

At 4:30am, many shops, schools and workplaces displayed the first copied posters about what was going on, giving advice on what to do. Most members of the social defence groups had designated areas of the city they were responsible for covering with posters, using special glue to make them a little more difficult to remove. Date, time, and place for the first public demonstrations were written on windows with spray cans or permanent markers.

At the same time the global networks of supporters were informed and asked to stage protests outside the embassies of the attacking power. Some networks had pre-arranged four digit codes for what activities they should take on. The code also informed the receiver of the attacker's identity. In most cases this would be publicly known; the message was just in case mainstream media were censored or shut down. Some people working in the media included the same codes in ads and articles.

When foreign troops crossed the borders, landed with aeroplanes, or reached harbours in the attacked country, the "documentation groups" collected photos and detailed information. At the same time the word went out to the organisers of public protests about where the invasion took place and foreign troops could be spotted. A special group that had planned to disrupt the use of the infrastructure met to see what could be done without harming necessary use of the roads, canals, harbours, electricity grid, railways, communication antennas and fibre optic cables for the local people. The overall motto when they made plans for this was to make it as difficult as possible for the invaders without serious harm to the local population.

Production facilities, media houses, police forces, educational institutions, hospitals, and local, regional and national administration each had their own plans for how to act. Theatres, cinemas, sport stadiums, chess clubs, the scouts, Red Cross groups, political parties, and trade unions all had prepared plans for a number of scenarios.

In the years of preparation, what to do openly versus what to keep secret was a topic of controversy. The traditional ideal of maximum openness within the nonviolent communities stood against the pragmatic view that opponents would be able to easily prevent acts of resistance if they knew what was going to happen. Since no consensus was reached, the resistance movement was using both strategies: most plans were made public while some remained secret. This fitted well with the decentralised organisational structure of the movement. All groups and individuals had a common overall goal and strategy, but each local and specialised action group was autonomous. In the same way a pyramid could symbolise the traditional structure of a military army or unit, a jazz session could be the symbol for the resistance: All agreed on the overall goals and strategies, but each player was expected to improvise and take initiatives when appropriate. Within the framework of the agreed overall plans, the preparations and training had encouraged individuals and groups to act based on their best judgement of the situation, their skills, and their gut feeling about what to do.

The result was that some groups had secret plans about which tactical techniques to use, whereas others had not tried to hide their preparations.

Since the first serious discussions of building a nonviolent force to protect the society, they had collected descriptions of "resistance tools" based on historical cases and constructed creative ideas still not tested in real struggle. These "toolboxes" were organised similarly to Wikipedia and open for everyone to use. They also had developed a system to avoid too many foolish and disruptive entries to be added. Some experienced activists had a collective editorial role. To prepare for a situation without access to the internet most organised groups and individuals in the resistance movement had frequently printed the most recent updates of the toolbox. Part of the regular trainings and preparations had been to arrange coordinated exercises in which many local groups practised a number of the resistance techniques from these toolboxes.

These exercises included training in how to avoid clashes and violent confrontations between the resistance groups as well as with domestic or foreign troops. Emphasis was also on what to do when accusations and suspicion of infiltrators spread among the activists. Keeping the movement united in a heated crossfire of false information, gossip, rumours and provocative behaviour had proven to be difficult for other movements in similar situations.

One central part of the strategy was to make a strong and united opposition as visible as possible. None of the domestic or international actors and observers should have any doubt that the population was united in opposing aggression. Another core strategy aimed at limiting the support for the invading forces. Whatever they needed from locals should be made as difficult as possible to access. Refusal to cooperate and sabotage of resources and infrastructure were part of the plans. Most of the population had their own storage of enough water, food, fuel and medicine for at least two months. In some cases, the storage was for a village or a neighbourhood, in other cases only for one household. All were drilled in how to use as few resources as possible and to be prepared to suffer as well as share when the situation became tough.

To keep the spirit of resistance alive when the situation became a serious burden was crucial. Cracks in the ranks had proven to be disastrous for other movements, so these issues were discussed during the exercises and trainings. It was essential to support those who needed help and to identify them as early as possible prior to a serious crisis.

Symbols of unity, cultural expressions and humour were important elements in keeping the mood strong. Studies of historical resistance movements had been part of the school curriculum for a decade and the young generation had the creativity and inspiration necessary to develop their own symbols, songs and skits. They knew that military and political elites had few weapons to use against a united population willing to risk the consequences of noncooperation and who could do it with a sense of humour.

In every resistance group there were people designated to document what they were doing and how they were met by other people and representatives from the occupier. Videos, photos, soundtracks and written reports were produced and circulated as widely and frequently as possible. Local and regional representatives evaluated these reports continually. Based on the conclusions, they proposed new tactical and strategic ideas to be discussed and implemented by the movement.

If the Internet was closed down, the documentation would be disseminated through other means of communication. USB-sticks with videos, photos and texts would be picked up in supermarkets, churches, sport stadiums, cinemas, schools and other places people visited frequently. Each receiver was asked to copy them and circulate them further. Deals were

11

done with crews on ships, pilots, bus and other drivers to bring copies to other cities and abroad.

As soon as the agreement was reached among the resistance groups to initiate actions, massive public protests and disruption of all but the essential functions of the society escalated quickly. None could avoid seeing the massive activities and getting the message. And for the invading troops the needed support from the local population would be almost nonexistent.

What's going to happen? Will the attackers give up and go home? Will they become ruthless against the resisters? Will international protest cause the leaders in the attacker country to lose their jobs? Will others be inspired by the resistance? Will other potential attackers rethink their plans?

There are various possible outcomes. It's a hypothetical scenario, and we don't propose a single conclusion to the story. What the scenario does illustrate is that a population can do a lot to organise itself to resist aggression – and do it without violence.

1
Introduction

Social defence is nonviolent community resistance to repression and aggression, as an alternative to military forces. "Nonviolent" means using rallies, strikes, boycotts and other such methods that do not involve physical violence against others. Social defence has other names, including nonviolent defence, civilian-based defence and defence by civil resistance.

The basic idea is to replace military forces and methods with a different sort of system, relying on unarmed civilians. Our aim is to describe the key elements of this alternative.

The word "defence" has largely been taken over by the military. Decades ago, governments had departments of war, but gradually "defence" became the standard name. "Defence" is a euphemism, because if militaries were only used for defence and never for attack, there would be no war or military-backed governments.

The possibility of defence by unarmed civilians was stimulated by observation of people's struggles against oppressive governments. In the mid 1800s, Hungarians were ruled by an emperor, part of the Austro-Hungarian empire. A nationalist movement developed, seeking greater independence and freedom. The movement did not use arms. Instead it used a variety of methods of noncooperation, including boycotting Austrian businesses, refusing to pay taxes, refusing to speak German and refusing to serve in the Austrian army.[1]

From 1898 to 1905, people in Finland mounted an unarmed resistance to the Russian empire, seeking autonomy. This struggle was mostly successful.[2]

If people can organise resistance to a repressive government and succeed without using arms, this suggests the possibility of replacing armed forces altogether. With suitable planning and training, people could be prepared to resist aggression without weapons.

---

1 Tamás Csapody and Thomas Weber, "Hungarian nonviolent resistance against Austria and its place in the history of nonviolence," *Peace & Change*, vol. 32, no. 4, 2007, pp. 499–519.

2 Steven Duncan Huxley, *Constitutionalist Insurgency in Finland: Finnish "Passive Resistance" against Russification as a Case of Nonmilitary Struggle in the European Resistance Tradition* (Helsinki: Finnish Historical Society, 1990).

During World War I, famous British philosopher Bertrand Russell wrote an article suggesting the possibility of defending Britain by noncooperation.[3] The idea was taken up by a number of authors in subsequent decades.[4] One of them was Stephen King-Hall, who had been an officer in the British navy in World War I. Just before the outbreak of World War II, King-Hall advocated a campaign using leaflets to undermine Hitler's rule in Germany. Unable to convince the British government to act, he began the campaign privately, and it caused considerable disturbance to the Nazis.[5]

King-Hall's book *Defence in the Nuclear Age* was published in 1958, at the height of the Cold War.[6] The US and Soviet governments had developed nuclear weapons and had them ready to use. To many, it seemed insane to threaten to kill millions of people in order to "defend" a country. King-Hall made an important point: the aim of defence should not be to protect a territory but rather to protect a way of life. For King-Hall, the way of life he deemed worth defending was British parliamentary democracy, with its associated freedoms. Not everyone would see British society in the 1950s as their highest ideal, but the point is more general: defence should be about values, not just lives and buildings.

If the aim of defence is to defend values, then all methods should be evaluated in terms of their effect on values. Nuclear war would be devastating. Furthermore, threatening to kill millions of foreign civilians undermines any claim to higher moral purpose: it might protect "us" from physical harm but at the expense of being implicated in mass murder.

Without weapons for defence, it might be possible for invaders to enter a country. But to conquer the country normally requires obtaining cooperation from a proportion of the population, in order for farms and factories to operate and for orders to be obeyed. If people are united in opposition, there are many ways to frustrate the goals of the invaders.

---

3 Bertrand Russell, "War and non-resistance," *Atlantic Monthly*, vol. 116, no. 2, August 1915, pp. 266–274. What Russell referred to as "non-resistance" would now be better described as noncooperation.

4 See the bibliography for key writings in the area.

5 Stephen King-Hall, *Total Victory* (London: Faber & Faber, 1941), pp. 209–211, 283–304.

6 Stephen King-Hall, *Defence in the Nuclear Age* (London: Victor Gollancz, 1958).

There is another factor, highlighted by King-Hall. If a country has no weapons, it does not pose a military threat to others. In particular, having no nuclear weapons reduces the risk of coming under nuclear attack. Given that nuclear war is the most devastating possibility, then "defence in the nuclear age," to refer to the title of one of King-Hall's books, must rationally be better when there is no incentive for enemies to attack using nuclear weapons. Having no armaments of any sort makes this threat remote.

Arms races, better labelled military races, involve an escalation in military preparedness involving two or more potential adversaries. They involve threat perceptions or, more commonly treat *mis*perceptions: the enemy is seen as dangerous, so greater military forces and preparedness are required to defend against attack. The so-called enemy sees things in exactly the same way, so both sides increase their capacities for war. A famous example

is the "missile gap." During the US presidential election in 1960, candidate John F. Kennedy claimed the US trailed the Soviet Union in nuclear-armed intercontinental ballistic missiles. Although informed that the US nuclear arsenal was actually more powerful, he persisted in his claims, discovering after being elected that the gap was non-existent and the US was ahead. One feature of military races is that leaders of governments can cement their own power by raising the alarm about enemies.

Getting rid of weapons undermines military races. How can more military expenditure be justified when the supposed enemy disarms and furthermore invites unlimited numbers of inspectors to verify that no weapons exist?

Enemies serve well to justify military establishments. They also provide a potent distraction from a key function of militaries: to defend rulers against their own people.[7] This is most obvious in military dictatorships, when generals run a country. More commonly, militaries are the tools or allies of governments in repressing opposition through force and terror. Even in societies with free elections and civil liberties, soldiers are called upon as a last resort to any popular uprising (violent or not). For example, if workers occupy workplaces, dispensing with bosses, the government may call in the troops.

This brings up the most common need for "defence": it is not against foreign invaders but rather against one's own government, when it uses force against citizens. Getting rid of armaments and armies and instead relying on

---

7 Militaries have other functions too, for example intervening in foreign wars, protecting economic investments and fostering the arms industry.

popular citizen action for defence is a threat to governments. If the people can resist a foreign invader, then they can use the same skills to resist the government itself.

The existence of militaries raises the old question, "Who guards the guardians?" One resolution to this question is for the people to be their own guardians.

Terms

As noted, there are various names for this alternative.
- Nonviolent defence
- Civilian defence
- Civilian-based defence
- Social defence
- Defence by civil resistance

"Nonviolent defence" makes clear that the defenders do not use violence, but the term "nonviolent" is not widely understood. Many people think it means being passive; it does not immediately bring to mind methods such as strikes, occupations and alternative government.

"Civilian defence" identifies the defenders as civilians, not soldiers. However, this term is easily confused with "civil defence," which is something different, referring to preparations to protect against bombings, for example underground shelters. The expression "civilian-based defence" overcomes this problem: the defence is based on actions by civilians. It is sometimes abbreviated CBD.

"Civil resistance" is an alternative term for "nonviolent action," so "defence by civil resistance" simply means defence by using the methods and approach of nonviolent action.

All these terms refer, in one way or another, to the defenders or their methods. Somewhat different from these is "social defence," which can be interpreted as either defence of society or the defenders being members of society.

We will most often refer to "social defence" if for no other reason than it is shorter and more convenient. We'll also use the other expressions at times, especially when discussing authors who use them in their writings.

Some writers see social defence as a replacement for military defence. In contrast, others see social defence as people's nonviolent resistance to domination, especially resistance to a government's repressive measures. In this second meaning, present-day campaigns, such as by feminists and workers, would be called social defence. We are open to both perspectives, but prefer to think of social defence as involving systematic planning and preparation for resistance.[8]

How it would work

The idea of defending a population against attack without using violence is unfamiliar to most people. Therefore it is difficult for them to conjure up a picture in their minds about how it might work. Another problem is that the power and ruthlessness of enemies are often inflated. The example of the Nazis often comes up. How could people defend themselves against Nazi invaders or occupiers without using violence?

Part of the problem is the assumption that the enemy is an alien force, ruthless, usually nameless, suddenly launching an invasion, like when the Nazis invaded Poland in 1939 and the Netherlands, Belgium and France in 1940. A first step in examining how social defence might work is to figure out the purpose of the rulers and commanders of the invading force. Do they want to impose a new ruler? Do they want to exploit the area's resources? Do they want to kill all the people?

To help answer such questions, it's useful to look at actual wars. Consider, for example, the war launched by the Iraqi government against Iran in 1980, the Malvinas/Falklands war of 1982, the Indochina wars from the 1940s to 1975, the wars in the Congo starting around 1996, and the wars associated with Daesh/Islamic State. These are very different in a number of ways, in terms of motivations, scale and dynamics. There are two commonalities, though.

First, in all these wars, all sides used arms. Therefore, they don't provide much guidance for what a war, or struggle, would look like if one side adopted social defence.

---

8 Wolfgang Sternstein, "Strategies of transition to social defense," *Civilian Based Defense: News & Opinion,* vol. 6, no. 1, July/August 1989, pp. 8–10, describes three transitions to social defence, involving "bridge builders" who want to make alliances with militaries and governments, "dam builders" who use campaigns from below to build the capacity for a social defence system, and "tunnel builders" who want to overthrow capitalism, the state and other forms of domination and then defend the new society nonviolently. Our approach is closest to the dam builders.

Secondly, in none of these wars was there a goal of killing everyone. The idea that aggressors are ruthless killers often underlies fears associated with not having military defence. One of the biggest obstacles to promoting social defence is people's fears about being subjected to a ruthless enemy.

Then there is genocide, which involves mass killing of an entire group, as for example in Bangladesh in 1971, Cambodia in 1975–1979 or Rwanda in 1994. Genocide can be considered to be a war against civilians.[9] Genocide nearly always takes place inside a country. It is a problem enabled by military forces. Social defence is a protection against genocide in two ways: it means getting rid of military forces and it gives people the capacity to resist.[10]

Prior interest in social defence

Stephen King-Hall was just one of several writers who raised the idea of social defence. In the following decades, there continued to be new contributions. Then, in the 1980s, with the huge expansion of the movement against nuclear war, groups interested in promoting social defence sprang up in several countries around the world, including Australia, Britain, France, Germany, Italy, Netherlands, Norway, Sweden and the US. We the authors were involved then, separately, Jørgen in Scandinavia and Brian in Australia.

However, after the end of the Cold War in 1989, interest in social defence declined drastically, as did involvement in peace action. Social defence had never been well known, but became even more obscure.

Writing in 1978 in an introduction to a special issue on civilian defence in the *Bulletin of Peace Proposals,* Nils Petter Gleditch wrote:

> In the twenty years or so of serious, concrete discussion of nonviolent defense alternatives, very little headway has been made. Governments have commissioned studies – but none have proceeded to the stage of implementation. ... No country has even been prepared to form a nonviolent branch of its defense forces.[11]

---

9 Martin Shaw, *What Is Genocide?* (Cambridge: Polity, 2007).

10 See chapter 9 for a response to the question "What about defending against genocide?"

11 Nils Petter Gleditch, "Civilian defense – from discussion to action?" *Bulletin of Peace Proposals,* vol. 9, no. 4, 1978, pp. 291–292, at p. 291.

That was over 40 years ago, and since then things are no more advanced: "very little headway has been made." Without pressure from campaigners, most governments have shown zero interest in nonviolent alternatives to military systems.[12]

We think social defence is just as important today as it ever was. The problems due to military forces continue to cause massive death, suffering and environmental impact. The usual approaches – such as international law, international peacekeeping and peace education – are worthwhile but do not get to the roots of the problem. Social defence offers a different way of addressing these problems, one that involves gradually eliminating military forces and developing the capacity for a different way of ensuring security against aggression and repression.

Rather than recount the history of the idea of social defence and the stories of relevant activism – this would be a worthwhile but mammoth task – we present here some basics about social defence, aimed at a new generation. For those who would like to explore the topic more deeply, in the bibliography we list a number of classic treatments. It would be possible to investigate these thoroughly and come up with many valuable suggestions. However, because social defence is still mainly an idea rather than a practical reality, there is just as much to be gained by trying ways to promote it and seeing what happens.

In this book

In the following chapters, we address a range of issues concerning social defence. We present some of the arguments why it is a worthwhile goal. However, we don't try to address every objection. Our treatment is oriented to readers who are open to the possibility of social defence and interested in knowing more about how it might work and how to move towards it.

We don't attempt to provide a blueprint for moving from today's military systems to future social defence systems. Because there is no experience in making such a transition, it is not sensible to predict or prescribe how this might occur. Instead, our emphasis is on ways that social defence, as a possible

---

12 In the early 1990s, governments in the newly independent countries Latvia, Lithuania and Estonia briefly showed interest in civilian-based defence, but then introduced conventional military forces.

goal, can be a guide for action, in social movements and beyond, helping campaigners to be more effective in empowering people. In addition, well-chosen actions today can help lay the groundwork for introducing social defence when, in the future, opportunities arise.

In chapter 2, we outline some of the main problems with military systems, including their horrific toll of death and destruction, their high cost, and their support for oppressive political and economic systems. The harmful aspects of military systems are so great that exploration of alternatives is easily warranted.

In chapter 3, we describe two historical episodes of nonviolent resistance to invasions and three cases of resistance to military coups, drawing out lessons for how a social defence might be set up. Our treatment of each of the histories is brief. Our purpose is not richness of detail but insights that can be transferred.

In chapter 4, we present more than 20 "ideas about social defence." Among other things, these ideas include what is being defended, how social defence can be organised, the effect of armed resistance, and the roles of planning, training and communication. These ideas about social defence are our views based on research or experience. They provide a starting point for understanding social defence and how to promote it, and also introduce some of the debates around social defence. These ideas are open to challenge and revision. Indeed, we hope others will question the ideas as well as build on and supplement them.

In chapter 5, we comment on technological and social developments in the past several decades, especially since the end of the Cold War in 1989. On the technological side, the rise of the Internet and the widespread uptake of social media have changed the communication scene dramatically, opening new opportunities for resistance to aggression but also enabling greater surveillance of social movements. On the social side, the emergence of terrorism as a rationale for military and national security systems has shifted the usual discourse about threats for which military responses are necessary.

In chapter 6, we comment on social movements and their connections with social defence. Currently, social defence as an organising focus is almost completely off the agenda. However, there are connections with several movements, most obviously the widespread commitment to nonviolent

21

action in environmental, peace, labour, feminist and other movements. We comment on what these movements have to gain by thinking in terms of social defence, and how this might happen in practice.

In chapter 7, we suggest some possible things you can do to help promote social defence, ranging from engaging in conversations to running simulations. We emphasise activities that are useful for everyday purposes, such as using secure communications and better understanding what makes people tick.

Chapter 8 tells about a nonviolent campaign against a nuclear waste site in Sweden, accompanied by our assessment of how this campaign contributed to promoting social defence. Chapter 9 gives our responses to some questions about social defence, for example "What about defending against genocide?" In chapter 10, we offer a few final thoughts.

2
The downsides of military systems

There are many harmful aspects of the system of using military force. The most important are the human cost and environmental damage from wars, the cost of military systems, and the militarisation of society. Militarisation refers to the adoption of military methods and thinking, and includes the glorification of soldiers and war, the creation and dehumanisation of the "enemy," the fostering of systems of command and obedience, and the use of the army to defend inequality and to repress dissent. On top of all this, military preparations are self-fulfilling: they trigger the very threats for which they are presumed to be the solution.

In this chapter, we give an overview of these negative features of military systems. Of course, there are also quite a few positive features, including deterring and defending against dangerous enemies, serving the community in natural disasters, and developing skills and discipline in soldiers. We've known quite a few members of military forces. Many of them are model citizens, being clear-thinking, highly skilled and dedicated to the service of the community. They care about others and are willing to risk their lives. Our concerns are not about individuals but about the military as a system.

Regardless of the net balance of positives and negatives of military systems, it is worth considering alternatives, because some alternatives may be better overall. In particular, we think social defence has much to recommend it.

What is being defended?

What are military forces for? In many people's thinking, they are for defence: defending a country against foreign attack. However, if all the world's militaries were only used for defence, they would never be used. There would be no wars or invasions because there would be no attacks.

This implies that the only attacks are by aggressive forces, and so military defence is needed by non-aggressive states to defend against the aggressive ones. In other words, the good guys need militaries to defend against the bad guys. The trouble with this argument is that leaders on both sides believe they are the good guys.

Another argument is that militaries are needed to deter aggression. The bad guys would attack but they don't because they know they will be met by force. This is the argument for nuclear weapons: they are needed to deter other governments from using their nuclear weapons, the result being what has been called Mutually Assured Destruction or MAD.

Yet another argument is that military forces are needed to intervene in other countries to ensure global security and stop threats from emerging. Interventions can also be claimed to promote justice and freedom.

Rather than taking the usual explanations at face value, another approach is to see them as justifications that hide or cover over more fundamental factors. In other words, the need for defence is mainly a pretext, not the real reason for having militaries.

Nearly half of the world's military spending is by one government, that of the United States. It is preposterous to think that this huge outlay is needed to defend against foreign invasion, namely to be used only for defence. Instead, it is important to note that US military forces have been deployed in numerous foreign wars, used to invade numerous countries, and are stationed in over a hundred foreign countries. It is convenient that in the US there is a deep-seated popular and political belief in the righteousness of the country's mission to help others.

It's also useful to remember the bloody history of Western colonialism, in which militaries from Spain, Portugal, France, Germany, Britain, Belgium, Netherlands and the United States conquered peoples in other parts of the world and ruled for decades or centuries. The role of the military for all this time was conquest and control. Colonial empires mostly ended only after World War II. It is illusory to believe that militaries were once used for bad purposes (colonialism) but now are used only

24

for good purposes. It is also illusory to imagine that the arms industry serves only good purposes.

A different perspective

There has been violence between humans in most societies. However, military forces like those throughout the world today are a recent phenomenon. Modern militaries arose with the rise of the modern state just a few hundred years ago.[13]

There are two legitimate questions to ask government leaders. What is it they want to defend? And does the defence system work as intended?

Many will automatically respond to the first question that what they want to defend is "the country." Seldom do we see a more nuanced answer or more specific one. What do we mean by "the country"? Is it territory, population, state institutions, buildings, means of production, banks, infrastructure, religious communities, trade unions, farmland, culture, nature, the state system, freedom, social institutions, social relationships or what? When such follow up questions are asked the reply frequently is: "All of it."

But there is no universal tool or system to defend all parts of a society. Any strategy for defence must make priorities about what is most important to defend and what is less important. There are strong connections between what is defended and how to do it. Few would argue that you can defend natural parks with nuclear weapons.

When it comes to the military means there are serious and very clear limitations to what they can defend. High ranking officers with war experience know this very well, although they seldom talk about it in public.

After a lecture at a British Regiment some years ago, Jørgen was invited to a dinner with a group of officers who, between them, had served in many wars since the 1980s. Their conclusion in private talks can be summed up as follows:

> Politicians give us orders to go to foreign countries and establish peace, democracy, respect for human rights, etc. Falklands,

---

13 Bruce D. Porter, *War and the Rise of the State: The Military Foundations of Modern Politics* (New York: Free Press, 1994); Charles Tilly, *Coercion, Capital, and European States, AD 990–1992* (Cambridge MA: Blackwell, 1992).

Afghanistan, Iraq, Serbia, and Libya are just a few of the recent examples. The problem is that they have trained and equipped us to kill and destroy! And we are damned good at doing just that. But you cannot build democracy by dropping bombs from high altitudes or respect for human rights with cruise missiles. Too many politicians seem to believe that military forces are some sort of universal tools that can deliver the political goals governments order them to. We know better.

For certain, quite a lot *cannot* be achieved with military means. Weapon systems are specifically designed and developed to destroy and kill! Many of the things they destroy and kill are the same objects and values that people expect them to defend, everything from artworks to education to compassion.

Harm

Militaries cause immense harm to humans and the environment. This is most obvious in wars. In the past century, perhaps 100 million people have died in wars. A much larger number were wounded. For survivors, many are highly traumatised. Some soldiers suffer post-traumatic stress disorder for decades afterwards.

War serves as a form of terrorism, in the sense that it strikes terror into the minds of those who are targets of shooting and bombing. Even those who are unharmed physically may suffer mentally from constantly being threatened with harm.

Soldiers are prime targets in war. Civilians also suffer, sometimes in greater numbers. Wars can lead to deprivation and hunger. Damage to vital facilities, such as water supplies, can contribute to disease outbreaks. During the sanctions on Iraq, from 1991 to 2003 – when there was little direct fighting – a million or more Iraqis, many of them children, died due to the combination of malnutrition and disease. The sanctions were enforced by military force.[14]

It is well documented through history that the noble goals used to justify wars are very seldom fulfilled.[15] The euphemism *collateral damage*

14 Geoff Simons, *The Scourging of Iraq: Sanctions, Law and Natural Justice*, 2nd ed. (Basingstoke: Macmillan, 1998).

15 Ian Bickerton, *The Illusion of Victory: The True Costs of War* (Melbourne: Melbourne University Press, 2011).

refers to unintended consequences of military operations. There are always unintended consequences when bombs, missiles and bullets are used. But after centuries of documentation of such events it does not make sense to use this as an excuse anymore. One way to measure collateral damage is to count the number of civilians killed in war. According to the international rules and conventions that limit the action of belligerents in a war (in short *Laws of War*) civilians are illegal targets in war. When civilians are harmed, we often hear perpetrators express regret about the *collateral damage.*

When the American AC-130 gunship shelled the Konduz hospital in Afghanistan in October 2015 at least 42 were killed and 30 injured.[16] Later, President Obama issued an apology and announced the US government would be making condolence payments to the families of those killed in the airstrike. This case received a lot of attention, but war crimes take place regularly in every war. Furthermore, military means are often used without a formal war being declared or recognised. The escalating use of drones has added to this development. Typically these attacks, especially the killing of civilians, receive little attention in the mass media. A major criticism of drone strikes is that they result in excessive collateral damage. Kilcullen and Exum wrote in the *New York Times* that, "Press reports suggest that over the last three years drone strikes have killed about 14 terrorist leaders. But, according to Pakistani sources, they have also killed some 700 civilians. This is 50 civilians for every militant killed, a hit rate of 2 percent – hardly 'precision'."[17]

A report from Department of Peace and Conflict Studies at Uppsala University claims that 90% of the victims in modern wars are civilians.[18]

16 David Smith, "Kunduz hospital attack: US forces did not act on MSF warnings for 17 min," *The Guardian,* 25 November 2015.

17 David Kilcullen and Andrew McDonald Exum, "Death from above, outrage down below," *New York Times,* 16 May 2009.

18 C. Ahlström and K.-Å. Nordquist, *Casualties of conflict: report for the World Campaign for the Protection of Victims of War* (Uppsala University, Department of Peace and Conflict Research [Institutionen för freds- och konfliktforskning], 1991).

This has been disputed by Eckhardt from Lentz Peace Research Laboratory who argued that "On the average, half of the deaths caused by war happened to civilians, only some of whom were killed by famine associated with war ... The civilian percentage share of war-related deaths remained at about 50% from century to century."[19]

Whatever the percentage, it is difficult to continue calling these causalities unintended. When the means used always lead to the death of many civilians then those using these weapons know what they are doing, or they are incompetent. This must change our views about the excuses from the perpetrators and the arguments used to explain away such war crimes. When the regularly documented effect is war crimes, anyone using such weaponry is implicated and to hide it by using terms like *collateral damage* is not good enough.

Environmental damage

Militaries cause immense damage to the environment. In wartime, bombing leads to massive destruction and leaves large quantities of pollutants. Even in so-called peacetime, militaries use vast quantities of resources. The world's militaries are major contributors to greenhouse-gas emissions and hence to climate change.[20]

From the devastating effects of chemical and biological weapons used in the Vietnam War through the nuclear winter scenario of the Cold War to the still largely uncatalogued effects of depleted uranium munitions and phosphor bombs, the negative environmental effects of militaries and wars have long been recognised. But this has never had a serious impact on discussions on military budgets in parliaments. It has been as if the military's role is forgotten in the environmental debate. Even when global warming took over the scene as the most serious threat to human existence, the role of the military slipped away from the central stage, or was deliberately excluded.

The UN climate negotiations that took place in Paris in November 2015 never discussed the single largest user of petroleum in the world. It was a strange omission, given that the US military alone is the world's single

---

19 William Eckhardt, "Civilian deaths in wartime," *Bulletin of Peace Proposals,* vol. 20, no. 1, 1989, pp. 89–98, at p. 97.

20 Marty Branagan, *Global Warming, Militarism and Nonviolence: The Art of Active Resistance* (Houndmills, Basingstoke: Palgrave Macmillan, 2013), chapter 1.

largest petroleum user and has been the main enforcer of the global oil economy for decades. When we add the emissions from other states' armies the fact that no states have to include the military emissions in their CO_2 budget is just incredible. It is a sign of powerful lobbying and being put above all other political priorities.

> The history of how the military disappeared from any carbon accounting ledgers goes back to the UN climate talks in 1997 in Kyoto. Under pressure from military generals and foreign policy hawks opposed to any potential restrictions on US military power, the US negotiating team succeeded in securing exemptions for the military from any required reductions in greenhouse gas emissions. Even though the US then proceeded not to ratify the Kyoto Protocol, the exemptions for the military stuck for every other signatory nation.[21]

Chemical weapons are more than a century old and were first used on a massive scale in WWI. They were used in several wars in Asia during the Cold War period and destroyed human life as well as nature. Agent Orange was sprayed over large areas of Vietnam, Laos and Cambodia in the 1960s and 1970s. Land and forests previously contaminated with Agent Orange have still not recovered – after 50 years! The human toll includes US military veterans as well as thousands of Vietnamese civilians. Legal battles for compensation continue in the US courts to this day. The Organisation for the Prohibition of Chemical Weapons has done important work in the establishment of the Chemical Weapons Convention, which entered into force in 1997. It has been ratified by 65 states.

Nuclear weapons are still regarded as central for the governments of the nine countries known to have them in their arsenal: USA, Russia, United Kingdom, France, China, India, Israel, Pakistan, North Korea. Many more are under the so-called "nuclear umbrella" and expect to be "defended" by friendly states in a conflict. Nuclear weapons states continue to develop new versions of their weapon systems and to update plans to use them. A global nuclear war could kill hundreds of millions of people, and possibly trigger a nuclear winter causing mass starvation.

---

21 Nick Buxton, "The elephant in Paris – guns and greenhouse gases," *Common Dreams*, 13 November 2015.

During the Cold War, the US and Soviet armed forces – and the other nuclear states – produced enormous amounts of hazardous wastes. The waste must be kept separate for at least 100,000 years according to EU rules (500,000 years according the US rules). From this perspective, we need to understand the impossibility of securing the waste for such a period of time. Jesus of Nazareth walked around in Palestine 2000 years ago, the first pyramid in Egypt was built less than 5000 years ago, the last ice age ended 10,000 years ago, and Neanderthals lived in Europe 30,000 years ago. To guarantee storage to last 100,000 years is not credible. The present so-called defence will create a serious threat to generations for as long as *homo sapiens* continues to exist.

As a result of naval accidents there are at least 50 nuclear warheads and 11 nuclear reactors littering the ocean floor.[22] Misunderstandings, misjudgements, and accidents due to technical or human errors can result in enormous consequences for life on Earth.

Cost

Militaries impose a huge economic cost on societies. The world military budget is well over a trillion dollars.

It is true that military research and development has a few spin-offs for civilian use, and that troops sometimes perform socially valuable functions such as disaster relief. However, most of the expenditure on the military is a drag on economies. There is no economic benefit from aircraft carriers or exploded bombs.

Wars cause immense damage to the built environment, requiring enormous cost and effort to repair or rebuild. Even when there are no wars, militaries chew up large amounts of resources that might otherwise be used for health, education and welfare.

Military research also has the damaging effect of pushing civilian research in military directions. The development of rifles efficient for killing has the spin-off effect, especially in the US, of fostering a civilian killing culture. Propaganda techniques pioneered for wartime have been adopted by advertisers. In these and other ways, military priorities lead to costly consequences well outside the military domain.

---

22 International Peace Bureau, "Nuclear weapons," http://www.ipb.org/nuclear-weapons/.

Do costly expenditures on the military lead to a lean and effective fighting force? Sometimes, but in many cases not. Because most military forces are seldom tested in war, they are prone to waste and corruption. There are numerous examples of massive waste in procurement, with billions of dollars spent on useless technologies, of giant pay-offs to corrupt politicians, and padding of budgets with unnecessarily expensive items.

The military budget is often a substantial part of the overall state budget. Not all economic systems make it easy to calculate how large a part it is, and different countries count military expenditures in different ways. How should health and welfare payments to veterans be counted? What about debts created to finance militaries and wars? Since no state has unlimited resources, there will always be political questions of what to prioritise. Ministries of defence have a long history of successfully arguing for their interests.

The total world military spending for 2017 amounted to $1.7 trillion, or about 2.2 per cent of total world gross domestic product.[23] If just some of what is currently spent on military forces were reallocated to realising the Sustainable Development Goals agreed by the United Nations, significant progress could be made.

Military incompetence

Military operations are plagued by incompetence. In every country, the military runs as a monopoly for armed defence and offence, and as a monopoly has little incentive to achieve the highest standards. Incompetent decisions by commanders are commonplace. This adds to the cost: a more efficient and competent military sector would be cheaper.

The Boer War, the Somme, Tobruk, Pearl Harbor, the Bay of Pigs: these are just some of the milestones in a century of military incompetence, of costly mishaps and tragic blunders. Are these simple accidents – as the "bloody fool" theory has it – or are they inevitable? Norman Dixon argues that there is a pattern to inept generalship, a pattern

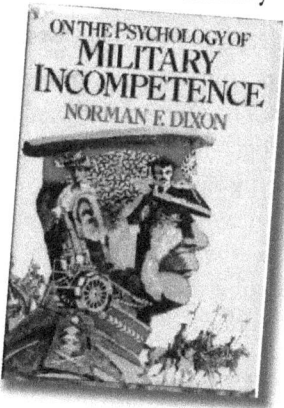

ON THE PSYCHOLOGY OF
MILITARY
INCOMPETENCE
NORMAN F DIXON

---

23 The Stockholm International Peace Research Institute provides lots of relevant information.

he locates within the very act of creating armies in the first place, which in his view produces a levelling down of human capability that encourages the mediocre and limits the gifted.[24]

Dixon published his book in the mid 1970s but examples of military incompetence did not end 40 years ago. In 2017 the former head of the Royal Navy, Lord West, told *The Independent* how British marines once accidentally invaded Spain while trying to land at Gibraltar in 2002.

> They charged up the beach in the normal way, being Royal Marines – they're frightfully good soldiers of course, and jolly good at this sort of thing – and confronted a Spanish fisherman who sort of pointed out, "I think you're on the wrong beach."

> And they all scrambled back in their boats and went away again. So I immediately had to get on to the Foreign Office and the governor of Gibraltar. The marines had in fact landed in La Linea, a Spanish town adjacent to Gibraltar. Juan Carlos Juarez, the town's mayor, said at the time: "They landed on our coast to confront a supposed enemy with typical commando tactics. But we managed to hold them on the beach."[25]

It is easy to smile at such a story, especially when it ended well. But just imagine what could happen if heavily armed units made mistakes like that in a different context and a tenser situation.

During the Cold War there were several incidents between East and West that occurred due to misunderstandings and incompetence. Submarines were close to colliding in the deep seas, civilian rockets were wrongly identified as military attacks, civilian passenger flights were shot down because they were believed to be military bombing squads.

Even worse are plans for using nuclear bombs on your own territory to prevent the enemy getting a foothold. Such exercises were made public in Norway after a NATO exercise included a scenario of attack from Soviet Union in which Norwegian officers in response decided to call for US

---

24 Norman Dixon, *On the Psychology of Military Incompetence* (London: Jonathan Cape, 1976).

25 Jon Sharman, "UK accidentally invaded Spain in 2002, reveals former First Sea Lord," *The Independent*, 4 April 2017.

fighters to bomb the northern region of Norway with nukes.[26] It is difficult to imagine defence incompetence worse than that!

Repression

Perhaps the most damaging consequence of military systems is their effect on society. In all sorts of ways, the military makes it more difficult to build a democratic, free and vibrant society.

Militaries are prime tools for repression. They are able to use violence to curtail free speech, movement and assembly.

This is most obvious in countries where the military actually runs the government or is used by the government to squash opponents and opposition. In some countries, criticism of the government is enough to warrant a prison sentence. In others, organising a protest rally or a strike may trigger arrests or murder.

In countries with repressive governments, the military is usually the ultimate protector of the rulers. Day-to-day control may be exercised by police, spies (surveillance operations), prisons and special forces, with the regular troops only deployed when routine control operations are insufficient. The role of the military is further in the background in countries where most people go along with government expectations.

Military means are in essence anti-democratic. As well as killing people, weapons destroy social networks, reduce respect for human rights, and lessen democratic institutions.

Even states generally regarded as democracies make decisions on war and military matters in authoritarian ways. When the Norwegian government agreed to join the US and other governments in bombing Libya in 2011, not even all in the government were part of the decision-making process. The Parliament was informed after the fighter planes were on their way and of course ordinary people had no say in this. In most cases the decisions to go to war are made by small groups of people behind closed doors and without a public debate where arguments in favour and against can be presented.

The military relies on the threat or use of violence. It is organised as a command system, with a strict hierarchy and the expectation of obedience to those with higher ranks. When these same characteristics pervade other

---

26 Kjetil Skogrand and Rolf Tamnes, *Fryktens likevekt: atombomben, Norge og verden: 1945–1970* (Oslo: Tiden, 2001).

parts of society, this is the process of militarisation, becoming more like the military. The result is that society is militarised, even in places where military forces play no direct role.

A militarised education system is a command system in which students are subordinate to teachers and teachers are subordinate to principals, and in which disobedience is severely penalised. Similarly, in the workplace bosses become commanders rather than leaders.

Glorification

A militarised society glorifies soldiers and military leaders, seeing them as models to be followed, especially when they die in battle. Histories emphasise wars and battles, especially victories, and downplay the virtues of cooperation, compromise, diplomacy and harmony.

History books are filled with descriptions of armed conflicts between and within states. The peaceful periods of good relations receive less attention. Fictional presentations of wars, such as movies, novels, and paintings, are also important in drawing attention to the violent phases of history. Most of it is presented in a nationalistic context, seldom providing an accurate description of the complexity of violent conflicts. But nonetheless, wars take up a huge part of our description of history.

The emphasis on the use of violence in conflicts can easily lead to the belief that violent conflicts are more common than good relations and unarmed handling of conflicts, and even suggest that wars are natural features of state relations. Actually, most conflicts in the world are solved without the use of violence, at all levels of conflicts: individual, group, local, regional, national and global. The reason many believe that conflicts and violence are almost interchangeable concepts is that most of the conflicts where one or more stakeholders use violence get attention and are documented. This goes all the way from interpersonal to global conflicts. Domestic violence gets attention and is documented by police, hospitals, social services, and in academic studies. In contrast, when a conflict between partners is resolved through lengthy discussion, mediation by a friend, having sex all night or any other nonviolent way, this is seldom reported, documented or studied by academics.

The same goes for conflicts between states. There are hundreds of books and thousands of articles documenting, describing, discussing and analysing the horrible violent break-up of Yugoslavia, but few on the peaceful division of Czechoslovakia. Media and textbooks give very biased descriptions of conflicts, with the bloodiest ones receiving the most attention. Peaceful ways to handle conflicts are neither reported nor recognised. The result is that many people do not distinguish violence from conflict. They do not identify the conflict or the many possible options, besides violence, for handling the seemingly incompatible goals of the parties involved.

This is bad enough for conflicts at homes, schools and workplaces. But when the conflict is between states and one of the best prepared tools to

handle it is the military, the consequences are even worse.

Despite the atrocities and the extreme suffering that follow so many deployments of the army, the majority of states still give a high priority to the military system. Many squares and boulevards are named after generals and state leaders who by any decent judgement are war criminals.

The French national anthem is a good illustration of how military violence is honoured. It starts like this:

Arise, children of the Fatherland,
The day of glory has arrived!
Against us tyranny
Raises its bloody banner
Do you hear, in the countryside,

The roar of those ferocious soldiers?
They're coming right into your arms
To cut the throats of your sons and women!

To arms, citizens,
Form your battalions,
Let's march, let's march!
Let the impure blood
Water our furrows!

And it just continues. From young school children to old age these words are sung frequently in France. It cannot happen without having an impact on people's views and identity.

The military propaganda penetrating our societies is a serious obstacle to a more open-minded discussion on how to handle conflicts.

Dehumanising the enemy

In a militarised society, enemies are seen as less than human or beyond reason: they are to be feared and hated rather than understood and reasoned with. If necessary, enemies are manufactured. Imaginary threats are used to justify military spending.

In order for soldiers to carry out killing operations, it is essential to dehumanise the people on the other side. In most wars, propaganda and training aim to make enemies seem less human than the soldiers on "our side."

In addition to calling them things like "cockroaches", "rats" or "gooks," one argument used is that they are first of all enemy soldiers who will kill "us." This line of arguing refuses to accept that soldiers are also human beings. We all have different roles and identities in our lives. Soldiers also have roles as fathers, football players, partners, daughters, chess enthusiasts, priests, builders and friends. Killing others means terminating all these roles. Killing cannot target only the roles that are problematic or a threat. By causing death to so many other roles, military killing in fact produces many more "enemies": the friends, colleagues and relatives of the dead soldier.

36

Self-fulfilling

There is a self-fulfilling aspect to military threats. Spending heavily on "defence" and running military "exercises" (dress rehearsals for battle) appears to foreign governments as preparation for attack, justifying their own military operations. This is a key feature of military races: militarism in one country encourages militarism in others.

Important military facilities are primary targets for any attacker. In case of a tense situation, conflict or open hostilities, the opponent will want to disable or destroy the other side's military capacities. The neighbourhood will be destroyed and people living in the vicinity will be in great danger as well as the intended military equipment, bunkers and buildings that are the primary targets. Military bases make the neighbourhood less safe!

All military forces have prepared lists of important targets to bomb in case of a conflict or war. It is only the locals who are unaware of the importance of bomb targets in their district.

The more military bases that are hosted in a country's territory, and the more important the bases are, the more probable they will be regarded as bomb targets by other states. Both for pre-emptive attacks and during an escalating conflict, all potential enemies will single out those targets that can do most damage in case of an open confrontation.

Internal control

Wars between governments are not that common compared to the use of militaries to control populations. The threat of external attack is used to justify internal repression. Alternatively, in civil wars, the threat from an internal enemy is used to justify repression. One of the most important functions of the military in any society is to hinder democratisation and greater equality.

This becomes most obvious when there is a serious challenge to the system. When workers take over a factory, sometimes troops are used to smash the power of the workers. In some famous revolutionary situations, such as the Paris Commune of 1871 and the Kronstadt sailors' strike in the Soviet Union in 1921, the army was deployed to crush the challenge to the government's control.

This brings up a more common role of the military: as a guarantor of the current system of rule, including economic inequality. Serious inequality has to be maintained by a strong belief system and, if necessary, the use of force. In capitalist countries, this is through protection of private property. No one could amass billions of dollars while others live in poverty without protection of the system that enables such inequality to develop and persist. Without the use of force, as an ultimate defender of the system and as a deterrent to challenge, collective action would be a possible threat to inequality.

Militaries thus serve as a serious brake on social change towards a more inclusive, just and equal society.

In many cases, the threat of an external enemy is the pretext for maintaining military preparedness. When there is any serious questioning of the military, there is the possibility of a threat of military intervention into civilian life, including a coup. Militaries have been likened to protection rackets, telling populations that payment is required, otherwise we may attack you.[27]

Militaries are closely connected to spy agencies, otherwise known as intelligence operations. Although some spying is undertaken against possible foreign enemies, much is directed towards domestic citizens, for the purposes of social control. In the United States, for example, there is a long history of secret operations by the FBI against peace activists and others seen as dangers – dangers to the government agenda. That peace activists could be seen as a threat is indicative of the military being seen as unquestionable.

The military-industrial complex

Militaries can become entrenched, which is why it is appropriate to call them systems rather than forces. Militaries involve troops and weapons – and much more, including military-oriented research and development, propaganda, industries geared to weapons production, education that inculcates beliefs favourable to the military, war memorials, veterans' groups and government expenditure on veterans' health. As well, there are all sorts of lobbyists, paid and unpaid, who attempt to influence politicians, industry leaders, educators, workers, film scriptwriters and others.

The connection between militaries and industries has been called the "military-industrial complex." It involves industries oriented to military

---

27 Charles Tilly, "War making and state making as organized crime," in Peter B. Evans, Dietrich Rueschemeyer and Theda Skocpol, eds., *Bringing the State Back In* (Cambridge: Cambridge University Press, 1985), pp. 169–191.

production, close connections between military leaders, politicians and business executives, and a myriad of links to groups that lobby for greater spending on the military. The "complex" typically involves more than just the military and industry, with the political and academic arenas often involved.

To talk of the military-industrial complex is one way of referring to militarism in a society. The values and goals of the military become diffused into various aspects of social life, and become so routine that they are not even noticed as anything special.

Military budgets need strong support and arguments to pass parliaments. To justify the huge amounts spent on the military, it is convenient to have an "enemy." During the Cold War the East and West used each other as justification for expanding their military budgets. After the Soviet Union collapsed and the Warsaw Pact dissolved, the argument for some years was that "it takes such a long time to build up a military defence that we cannot disarm and wait for a new enemy to appear before we spend more money on the military again." Then came the "Muslim threats" almost as a gift to the military establishment. Since "Muslims" did not plan to invade "our" countries with standing armies we saw the emergence of the use of armies for "international operations" as a main argument. Under the cover of "helping people and states," armies have been bombing and occupying other states that are not threats to the attacking states.

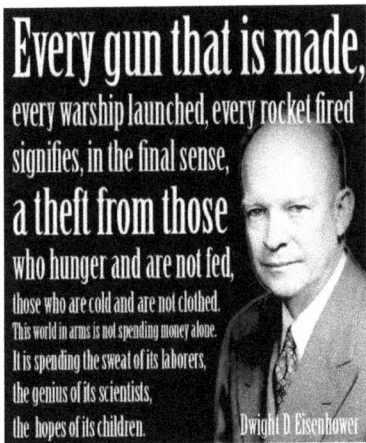

> Every gun that is made, every warship launched, every rocket fired signifies, in the final sense, a theft from those who hunger and are not fed, those who are cold and are not clothed.
> This world in arms is not spending money alone.
> It is spending the sweat of its laborers, the genius of its scientists, the hopes of its children.
>
> Dwight D. Eisenhower

After Obama took office in 2009, the US military increasingly used drones to kill and attack targets in countries around the world. By killing on the spot, the US government avoids taking the prisoners, something that troubled George W. Bush in his presidency. It does not make the strategy less of a war crime, but remote killing is less visible and disturbing for domestic policies. All major military armies are today following this path of spending more money on high tech weaponry that can be used with fewer risks for their own soldiers.

This leads us to the so-called "war on terror" since 2001. The threat of terrorists attacking "our" citizens has been used to expand not only military budgets but also a huge "security sector" that includes military, police, secret services, intelligence, surveillance, private companies and academia. There has been a militarisation of everything from airport controls to "peace studies" programs at universities. They all follow the money and adopt their arguments and applications to the widespread fear of "terrorists."

The latest development has been a militarisation of what the media call the "refugee crisis." And by that they mean crises for the societies where the refugees seek refuge. The real crisis is of course for the refugees. Military units and equipment are today used to prevent refugees from fleeing life-threatening situations and entering into territories they hope will give them some degree of safety.

Militaries not needed

History shows us that military means are frequently used to attack rather than to defend. With lies and distorted descriptions of reality, armies have attacked other states under the pretext of defending. Well documented examples of pretexts for attacks are the 1964 Tonkin Gulf incident used to justify the escalation of US attack on Vietnam[28] and the claim that Saddam Hussein had weapons of mass destruction in Iraq.

Since the establishment of the state system, military means have been regarded as the sharpest, best or even the only option for state leaders who want to use resources to "defend" themselves. When states have a limited number of tools for handling conflicts it should be no surprise that they use them from time to time. There is a whole military-industrial-media complex working to promote this way of handling conflicts, with far more resources and connections than anyone with a different view.

Not every state has a military. Costa Rica is often mentioned as the exception to the rule that every state needs an army. Barbey lists 26 states without an army, 23 of them members of United Nations General Assembly.[29]

---

28 Daniel Ellsberg, *Secrets: A Memoir of Vietnam and the Pentagon Papers* (New York: Viking, 2002).

29 Christophe Barbey, *Les pays sans armée* (Cormagens: Pour de Vrai, 1989); Christophe Barbey, *Non-militarisation: Countries without Armies* (Åland, Finland: Åland Islands Peace Institute, 2015). The countries are Andorra, Cook Islands, Costa Rica, Dominica, Grenada, Haiti, Iceland, Kiribati, Liechtenstein, Marshall Islands, Mauritius, Micronesia (Federated State of), Monaco, Nauru, Niue, Palau, Panama, Samoa, San Marino, Solomon Islands, Saint Kitts and Nevis, Saint Lucia,

That is close to 12% of the UN members. However, most of them rely on powerful neighbours or alliances for protection in case of attack.

These are in most cases small in territory and population. It seems that "small is beautiful"[30] when it comes to states: historically, in most cases smaller states have done less harm than huge empires. In most states the army is such a powerful, symbolic and important part of the self-image of a state that few can imagine alternatives.

Just wars?

The theory that some wars are "just" is based on the idea that they are "means of last resort." When all other "peaceful" options have been tried and have failed to produce the needed result, then the use of military means is justified. Most of the literature and discussions on just war theory argue that under attack the state can use violent means to defend territory, people, institutions and statehood.

The exclusion of nonviolent means for defence is a serious weakness in the discussion. The adherents to this theory present a false dichotomy between acquiescence and violence, not considering the use of nonviolent action as a way to both deter and prevent attack. As Gene Sharp has argued, "nonviolent struggle, sometimes also called people power, political defiance, nonviolent action, non-cooperation or civil resistance,"[31] is a possible alternative that removes the dichotomy and points to a very different conclusion than provided by just war theory.

In this book we use the term "social defence." This indicates that the defence is for and by society rather than the state. Social institutions, networks, stakeholders, and actors are more central both as values to defend and as those who can carry out the defence. Just-war discussions become more or less irrelevant when social defence replaces military systems.

Saint Vincent and the Grenadines, Tuvalu, Vanuatu, Vatican City State.

30 We allude here to E. F. Schumacher's famous book *Small is Beautiful: A Study of Economics as if People Mattered* (London: Blond & Briggs, 1973).

31 Gene Sharp, "Beyond just war and pacifism: nonviolent struggle towards justice, freedom and peace," *The Ecumenical Review,* vol. 48, no. 2, 1996, p. 233–250.

Conclusion

The rationale for military forces is that they protect societies from dangerous enemies. Yet militaries are responsible for a great deal of death and suffering, and commonly are used to repress and control the people they are supposed to be defending.

The downsides of military systems include high cost, the death and destruction of wars, the fostering of military races, and the orientation of social life to military thinking and methods. Militaries are a major restraining force on greater democracy and equality, usually being deployed in defence of rulers rather than the ordinary people.

It is important to remember that nearly all people involved with the military – rank-and-file soldiers, workers in arms manufacturers, surveillance experts, not to mention cooks, cleaners, engineers and lawyers – are well meaning. Many of them are kind hearted. The problem is not with the people involved in the military system, but with the system itself.

Military means are badly designed for defending what most people care about. When used, they do so much damage to human life, nature, infrastructure and civil society that the question "Is it worth it?" has an obvious answer.

There is a need for realistic, sustainable and less harmful alternatives to defend us from danger. When the defence system itself for centuries has created more problems than it solves, it is time to seriously discuss other options. One justification for the military is that there is no alternative. Actually, though, there are. Social defence is one of them.

3
Historical cases

No society has ever comprehensively organised itself for nonviolent resistance to aggression, and in this sense there are no historical cases of social defence in operation. However, there are some suggestive examples involving spontaneous nonviolent resistance to invasions and coups.

We summarise the cases of Czechoslovakia 1968 and Germany 1923, the two most prominent cases of nonviolent resistance to invasion and occupation. With advanced preparation, the resistance in each case might have been even more effective.

We discuss three important cases of nonviolent resistance to coups: Germany 1920, France-Algeria 1961 and the Soviet Union 1991. A coup is a sudden and illegitimate takeover of a government. Some coups are bloodless: they do not involve force. Others involve military force against resisters, especially when a segment of a country's military tries to take power, overthrowing the government, while other parts of the military remain loyal to the government. Over the past century, there have been hundreds of coups around the world. Some were successful; others were attempted but unsuccessful. Some countries have had one coup after another. Out of all these events, we describe three instances in which citizen action played a crucial role in stopping coups.

These historical examples give some pointers to the power of citizen action against invasions and coups, and ways to make it more effective, especially with planning and preparation. Our summaries here are not intended to provide comprehensive accounts of events, all of which involved many complications, but rather to highlight some of the actions relevant to social defence. Many previous treatments of social defence have discussed these same historical examples.

It would also be possible to choose some cases in which nonviolent methods were used against invasions and coups, but less successfully. For example, in several countries occupied by Nazi Germany during World War II, there was effective nonviolent resistance.[32] However, there was no

---

32 Jacques Semelin, *Unarmed Against Hitler: Civilian Resistance in Europe 1939-1943* (Westport, CT: Praeger, 1993).

significant nonviolent resistance to the original invasions and occupations because the population relied on military defence, which was unsuccessful. When there is an invasion or coup, the most common response by the civilian population is acquiescence. There is less to learn from such examples.

We present the five cases of invasions and coups in chronological order, so the first two involve Germany.

The Kapp Putsch[33]

World War I, called at the time the Great War, was primarily a European war. On one side were the Central Powers of Germany and Austria-Hungary and on the other were the Allies – Britain, France and Russia, with others

joining later. The war concluded in late 1918 when the German government surrendered. Afterwards, Germany had its first ever parliamentary democracy, called the Weimar Republic. It faced many challenges.

Within the military, a key source of grievance was forced reductions

---

33 Erich Eyck, *A History of the Weimar Republic* (Cambridge, MA: Harvard University Press, 1962), pp. 147–160; D. J. Goodspeed, *The Conspirators: A Study of the Coup d'État* (London: Macmillan, 1962), pp. 108–143; S. William Halperin, *Germany Tried Democracy: A Political History of the Reich from 1918 to 1933* (New York: Thomas Y. Crowell, 1946), pp. 168–188; John W. Wheeler-Bennett, *The Nemesis of Power: The German Army in Politics 1918–1945* (London: Macmillan, 1961), pp. 70–82.

in troop strength, required by the peace treaty in which the victorious Allies imposed many penalties and requirements. In 1919, military figures began plotting a coup to restore the monarchy. They were spurred into action by the Allies' demand for the trial of nearly 900 alleged war criminals, causing outrage throughout Germany. On 13 March 1920, commanders supporting a military takeover led troops into Berlin, the capital, to take control. The leader of the new regime was Wolfgang Kapp. The saga is called the Kapp putsch, a putsch being a coup d'état, namely a seizure of political power by the military.

Prior to this, General Hans von Seeckt, the Chief of Staff of the German army, told the Minister of Defence and a group of generals that "Troops do not fire on troops": this meant the government did not have the support of its own army commanders. Cabinet ministers left Berlin just an hour before the arriving rebel troops. Before departing, the ministers issued a proclamation calling for a general strike against the coup.

In Berlin, the government's call for a strike was accepted enthusiastically. Workers shut down everything: electricity, water, restaurants, transport, garbage collection, deliveries. It was the largest general strike in history to that time.

Civilians shunned Kapp's troops and officials, who could not get anything done. For example, Kapp issued orders, but printers refused to print them. Kapp went to a bank to obtain funds to pay the troops, but bank officials refused to sign cheques.

> A government needs money not only to make war, but also to carry out rebellion; and so Kapp asked the Reichsbank for 10,000,000 marks. But the officers of the bank would honor only the order of an authorized official and no such signature was to be had. For all the under-secretaries in the ministries refused to sign, and it did not seem to the cashier of the Reichsbank that the signature of "National Chancellor Kapp" offered quite the financial security required.[34]

The elected government, from its temporary location in Stuttgart, encouraged resistance. President Friedrich Ebert made a passionate appeal to the troops to oppose the coup; in leaflet form, this appeal was dropped by plane over

---

34 Eyck, *History of the Weimar Republic*, pp. 151–152.

barracks of the rebels' troops, while strikers passed copies directly to troops.

Kapp's planning was weak, and in power he was indecisive. According to one historian, "The Kapp *Putsch* was a triumph of ineptitude, infirmity of purpose, and lack of preparedness."[35] On the other hand, the government was weak and was widely (and falsely) blamed for Germany's defeat in the war.

In less than five days, Kapp gave up and fled from the country. Not a single shot had been fired against him in Berlin.

Kapp at one point ordered troops to shoot all the strikers, but the troops did not obey; if they had, the outcome might have been different. In other circumstances during the coup attempt, rebel troops shot and killed quite a few civilians.

Several features of the failed Kapp putsch are worth noting in relation to social defence. First, the resistance was spontaneous: there had been no advance preparation. It is reasonable to suppose that with preparation and training, the resistance could have been more effective and able to oppose a more competently organised coup. Second, in Berlin the population was unified in its opposition and used nonviolent methods only. Third, noncooperation was the primary method used, and it was effective because it was used so comprehensively. When bank officials refused to cooperate, this was in the context of everyday activities that we seldom think of as vital for resisting a military takeover. Today, a different set of workers would be involved, for example television technicians and computer specialists. Remember, the Kapp putsch occurred before both radio and television. For rulers to get anything done, they need all sorts of workers to do their jobs. The resistance to the Kapp putsch illustrates how powerful noncooperation can be.

There is another side to the putsch. Emboldened by the call for a general strike, tens of thousands of left-wing workers took control of several cities throughout Germany, and in Berlin the revolutionary Spartacists appeared on the streets. This time, though, General von Seeckt, who had been reluctant to oppose a right-wing attack on the government, was quite willing to use the army to suppress a left-wing challenge. Some of the troops used to smash the Communist uprising were the same ones that had marched into Berlin to launch the Kapp putsch.

35 Wheeler-Bennett, *Nemesis of Power*, p. 77.

The Ruhr, 1923[36]

After World War I, the victorious Allies imposed harsh penalties on the defeated governments. One key penalty was years of payments called reparations.

On several occasions, the German government defaulted on its payments, in part due to economic crisis, of which extreme monetary inflation was a prominent feature. Using the default as a pretext, in January 1923 French and Belgian troops occupied the Ruhr, a highly populated and heavily industrial part of Germany bordering France. The British and US governments did not favour this action but did not try to stop it. Leaders of the French government also sought to prevent the recovery of the German economy and possibly to annex the Ruhr.

The people living in the Ruhr opposed the occupation, but there was no prospect of military resistance. The occupation generated enormous outrage throughout Germany, uniting the otherwise highly divided country. The German government called on its citizens to resist the occupation by what was called, at the time, "passive resistance," namely resistance without physical violence.

The key resistance tactic was to refuse to obey orders from the French occupiers. This was costly: thousands who ignored orders were arrested and tried by military tribunals, which handed out heavy fines and prison sentences. There were also protests, boycotts and strikes.

The resistance had many facets. The French demanded that owners of coal mines provide them coal and coke. When negotiations broke down, the German negotiators were arrested and court martialled. This generated an enormous response throughout Germany: support for the accused came in the form of telegrams and delegations. After the six accused were fined heavily, they were feted on return to the city of Essen.

---

36 Wolfgang Sternstein, "The *Ruhrkampf* of 1923: economic problems of civilian defence," in Adam Roberts (ed.), *The Strategy of Civilian Defence: Non-violent Resistance to Aggression* (London: Faber and Faber, 1967), pages 106–135. For a wider perspective, addressing the German government's diplomacy in the ending of the resistance and its damaging effect on German democracy, see Barbara Müller, *Passiver Widerstand im Ruhrkampf: Eine Fallstudie zur Gewaltlosen Zwischenstaatlichen Konfliktaustragung und ihren Erfolgsbedingungen* (Münster: Lit, 1995).

Civil servants resisted. The German government said they should refuse to obey instructions from the occupiers. Some civil servants were tried for insubordination and given long prison sentences. Others were expelled from the Ruhr; over the course of 1923 nearly 50,000 civil servants were expelled.

Transport workers resisted. The French-Belgian occupiers tried to run the railways. Only 400 Germans agreed to work for the new administration, compared to 170,000 who worked in the railways prior to the occupation.

> As the German railwaymen left, they removed name plates, signal plans and installations, sabotaged tracks and rolling stock, or ran the trains into unoccupied territory. The French tried to requisition railway engines at the Rheinmetall works, but the workers sabotaged the engines by removing vital parts. They blocked the tracks with heavy pieces of iron, so that it was impossible to get even a single engine out. The French arrested the directors of the plant, who received heavy sentences and fines at a court martial. The mayor of Oberhausen, an important railway junction, caused the station's electricity to be cut off. He was arrested, tried, and banished to unoccupied Germany, and two of his successors were in turn treated in the same way for the same offence. When the French company finally succeeded in running a few trains, they were boycotted by the population. Shipping on the Rhine came to a complete standstill.[37]

In response to resistance by the press, the occupiers issued some 200 bans on newspapers. To get around this censorship, some large firms published news sheets for their workers, and newspapers from unoccupied Germany were smuggled into the Ruhr. There was also resistance from other groups, including shopkeepers and trade unions.

The resistance went on for months, but eventually broke down. The German government was in such dire economic straits that it was unable to continue providing financial support for impoverished resisters in the Ruhr. The government had to agree to end the struggle.

However, by this time the resistance, and the desperate situation of people in the Ruhr, had turned public opinion in Britain, the US and even in Belgium and France, in favour of the Germans. After the report of an

---

37 Sternstein, pp. 115–116.

independent international commission (the Dawes Commission), Germany's reparation debt payments were reduced and French troops were withdrawn. The resistance had failed in its immediate aims but was instrumental in blocking the wider aim of the French government to subordinate the German economy and maybe even dismember the country.

The German military, having been recently defeated in war, was in no position to offer armed opposition to the occupation: it would have been defeated again. The key to the effectiveness of the resistance was remaining nonviolent.

Along with noncooperation, some resisters used violent sabotage, for example blowing up railway lines and canal locks. This hindered the occupiers, who responded with brutal reprisals against uninvolved German

civilians. In one incident, saboteurs destroyed a railway bridge, causing the death of ten Belgian soldiers travelling in a train, and injury to many others. Reprisals against German civilians were brutal and sometimes lethal. Furthermore, the sabotage attack led to international denunciations. Overall, the more destructive forms of sabotage probably didn't help the immediate resistance very much while reducing sympathy for it.

As noted, the main resistance method was noncooperation, so the occupiers were frustrated in achieving their goals. Actually, it might have been more effective to do more in terms of fraternisation. As it was, many French troops, who had been subject to war propaganda about the subhuman Germans, actually found they were ordinary people struggling in difficult circumstances. Attitude changes among troops were part of what undermined the resolve of the French government.

The unity of the resistance was crucial. Likewise, the role of the German government proved vital: it supported nonviolent methods, giving them legitimacy, and it maintained this support through most of the struggle.

The Algerian Generals' Revolt[38]

The African country Algeria was colonised by France, and there were many French people living in Algeria. Within France, Algeria was considered to be not a colony but actually part of France.

In 1954, Algerian nationalists began an armed struggle for independence, which was met with brutal force by the French military. The bloody war ended up causing the deaths of perhaps a million Algerians out of a population of eight million. In 1961, French President Charles de Gaulle indicated that he would enter into negotiations with Algerian nationalists. In Algeria on the night of 21–22 August, four French generals who opposed negotiations launched a coup. There was even a possibility of an invasion of France. There were far more French troops in Algeria than in mainland France.

There was massive popular opposition to the revolt. After a couple of days of indecisiveness, De Gaulle went on national radio and called for resistance by any possible means. In practice all the resistance was nonviolent. There were huge protests and a general strike. People occupied airstrips to prevent aeroplanes from Algeria landing.

The resistance within the French military in Algeria was even more significant. The rebels in Algeria had taken control of radio networks, but they did not control broadcasting from France. Many troops in Algeria had transistor radios and heard, or heard about, De Gaulle's call to resist. Many French troops were conscripts and, especially after hearing de Gaulle's

---

38 Adam Roberts, "Civil resistance to military coups," *Journal of Peace Research*, vol. 12, 1975, pp. 19–36. For a blow-by-blow account, see Paul Henissart, *Wolves in the City: the Death of French Algeria* (St Albans, Hertfordshire: Paladin, 1973).

statement, opposed the coup. Many of them simply refused to leave their barracks. Another form of noncooperation was deliberate inefficiency, for example losing files and orders, and delaying communications.

Many pilots flew their planes out of Algeria and did not return. Others feigned mechanical breakdowns or used their planes to block airfields. The level of noncooperation was so extensive that within a few days the coup collapsed.

This was a highly successful nonviolent resistance to a military takeover. Various methods were used, including protests, occupations (of airstrips) and noncooperation by troops. It was crucially important that de Gaulle, as president, made a strong statement against the coup and supported popular action. This helped foster unity among the resistance. Dissent within the French military in Algeria was crucial to the opposition. The collapse of the Algerian Generals' revolt shows how noncooperation, including within the military, can be effective in opposing a coup. It was also important that the resistance remained nonviolent because this deprived the rebels of a pretext for initiating violence. The coup failed without a single shot fired against it.

Czechoslovakia 1968[39]

The Cold War was the confrontation between socialist and capitalist countries that lasted from about 1947 to 1989. Czechoslovakia, a country in Eastern Europe, was ruled by a Communist Party government and was part of the Warsaw Pact, a military alliance dominated by the government of the Soviet Union. This was decades before Czechoslovakia peacefully divided into Slovakia and the Czech Republic.

Although the countries in Eastern Europe were subordinate to the Soviet government, there was opposition. In 1956 in Hungary, there was an uprising against Communist rule, which was ruthlessly repressed. In

---

39 Royal D. Hutchinson, *Czechoslovakia 1968: The Radio and the Resistance* (Copenhagen: Institute for Peace and Conflict Research, 1969); H. Gordon Skilling, *Czechoslovakia's Interrupted Revolution* (Princeton, NJ: Princeton University Press, 1976); Jacques Semelin, *Freedom over the Airwaves: From the Czech Coup to the Fall of the Berlin Wall* (Washington, DC: ICNC Press, 2017); Tad Szulc, *Czechoslovakia since World War II* (New York: Grosset & Dunlap, 1971); Joseph Wechsberg, *The Voices* (Garden City, NY: Doubleday, 1969); Philip Windsor and Adam Roberts, *Czechoslovakia 1968: Reform, Repression and Resistance* (London: Chatto and Windus, 1969).

Czechoslovakia, the opposition was different. It was a reform movement within the country's Communist Party, largely supported by the population, to relax the harsh control measures typical in Eastern Europe. It was called "socialism with a human face." Referring to the capital city, it was also called the "Prague spring," suggesting a rebirth after a winter of bleak Communist rule.

However, this reform movement was unwelcome to the Soviet leaders. On 20–21 August 1968, half a million Warsaw Pact troops, mostly from the Soviet Union, invaded Czechoslovakia. The plan was to take over and quickly install a puppet government subordinate to Soviet control.

The Czechoslovak military was not prepared for this sort of attack. All its preparations were for defending against military attack from the West, from forces of NATO, the North Atlantic Treaty Organisation, the military alliance of capitalist powers, including the United States. In the face of the massive invasion, Czechoslovak military leaders decided not to resist because it would have been futile. Military defence would have been crushed within a few days.

Instead, though, there was a spontaneous civilian resistance. Tanks rolled into Prague and other cities without any military obstacles. So what did the resistance look like?

Initially, some Czechoslovaks threw garbage at invading troops and tried to set armoured vehicles alight, disabling many of them. In response, some of the troops opened fire, leading to casualties. However, most of the resistance did not involve violence.

There were huge demonstrations. There was a one-hour general strike on 22 August. Graffiti, posters and leaflets were used to publicise the resistance. A few individuals sat down in front of tanks. Farmers and shopkeepers refused to provide supplies to the invading troops. Staff at Prague airport cut off central services.

The Czechoslovak radio network allowed synchronous broadcasting from many locations across the country. It was controlled by the resistance and played a crucial role. The radio broadcast messages urging peaceful opposition. It also provided practical information about troop movements.

The Soviets brought in radio-jamming equipment by train. When this information was broadcast, workers held up the train at a station. Next it was stopped on the main line due to an electricity failure. Finally it was shunted onto a branch line where it was blocked by locomotives at both ends.

When the Soviets managed to identify a broadcasting studio and shut it down, broadcasting was continued from another city. In Prague, broadcasting equipment was regularly moved to different places. Across the country, broadcasts switched every 10 minutes between 12 different regional stations, on a two-hour cycle, to prevent the Soviets detecting their location.

The KGB, the Soviet secret police, had lists of people to arrest. The Czechoslovak secret police, who supported the resistance throughout, learned that the KGB planned to make mass arrests and leaked this information to the radio network. Announcers told how to avoid detection, harm and arrest, including details of when particular individuals were being hunted. To make the KGB's job more difficult, citizens removed house numbers and took down or covered over street signs. The radio network also announced the licence numbers of KGB vehicles. The accuracy of the radio broadcasts helped to reduce the role of rumours and false information.

An effective part of the resistance involved local people talking to the invading soldiers, engaging them in conversation, explaining why they were protesting. Some soldiers had falsely been told there was a capitalist takeover in Czechoslovakia; some of them thought they were in Ukraine or East Germany. When they learned that actually the opposition was socialist, many of them became "unreliable": they became sympathetic to the resistance and had to be replaced. For the invading troops, the combination of being met with strong arguments while being refused food and normal social relationships was upsetting, possibly leading some troops to be deliberately inefficient. Because troop loyalty was undermined, Soviet leaders were reluctant to impose direct military rule.

Language skills were important. The local languages were Czech and Slovak, but after the Communist Party took power in 1948, students were required to learn Russian at school, so they were able to speak to Russian soldiers. So imagine some young Soviet soldiers, perhaps 20 years old, conscripted into the army and being sent to invade Czechoslovakia, told they are defending socialism. They are met by young students, also around 20 years old, telling them that they were socialists too. This was the human side of the resistance, a person-to-person interaction called fraternisation.

Czechoslovak political leaders supported the resistance but did not try to coordinate it. President Svoboda refused to bring in a new government. The Czechoslovak Communist Party held an underground meeting under the noses of the occupying forces; the radio network was used to inform delegates about it. Alexander Dubcek, secretary of the Communist Party and the most visible leader of the reform movement, maintained his position. The resolutions of the meeting, fully supporting the resistance, were broadcast by the radio network. This was important symbolically: the people and their leaders were united. This meant the Soviets were unable to quickly set up a puppet government.

Dubcek, Svoboda and other Czechoslovak political leaders were arrested and held in Moscow. Under severe pressure and without communication with the resistance back in Czechoslovakia, they made unwise concessions.[40] They didn't realise how widespread and resolute the resistance was. The leaders' concessions deflated the resistance, so its active phase lasted only a week. However, it took another eight months before a puppet government could be installed in Czechoslovakia.[41]

The resistance thus failed in its immediate aims. However, it was immensely powerful in its impacts. The use of force against peaceful citizens undermined the credibility of the Soviet Communist Party. At this time, most countries around the world had communist parties, some of them quite strong and most looking to the Soviet party for leadership. The Prague spring changed all this. Many foreign communist parties splintered, with

---

40 Jaroslav Sabata, "Invasion or own goal?" *East European Reporter*, vol. 3, no. 3, Autumn 1988, pp. 3–7; Semelin, *Freedom over the Airwaves,* pp. 124–127.

41 The full story is complex. For a detailed account of political machinations, see Szulc, *Czechoslovakia since World War II.* We have highlighted here points relevant to social defence.

some members quitting or the parties splitting into old guard supporters of the Soviet line and supporters of the reform approach.

Because the resistance was nonviolent, Soviet propaganda was less effective. Indeed, the invaders staged some incidents purportedly showing the Czechoslovaks using violence.

And what about Western governments that were armed to the teeth to oppose the possibility of an invasion from the Warsaw Pact? They mouthed criticism of the invasion but did nothing practical. Neither was there any support from the United Nations.

For proponents of social defence, what can be learned from the 1968 struggle in Czechoslovakia? The first and most obvious lesson is that remaining nonviolent has a powerful effect in discrediting the aggressor – as long as outsiders have a clear picture of what was happening.

The Czechoslovak resistance was spontaneous, so it cannot really be considered to represent the operation of a social defence system. No one was trained for resistance and no technological systems were specifically designed for resistance. Despite these limitations, the opposition was surprisingly effective. It can only be imagined how much more effective it might have been with systematic preparation.

Fraternisation was important. To enable effective interaction with invaders, learning languages, understanding cultural factors and having opportunities to interact were all important.

Communication systems were crucially important, especially the radio network. Broadcasts telling of the nonviolent resistance undermined Soviet propaganda claiming the invasion was necessary to maintain socialism. Designing communication systems is a vital part of a social defence system.

The Czechoslovak people were almost entirely united in opposition, and united also with the Czechoslovak Communist Party. This made it far easier to maintain nonviolence and to oppose the imposition of a Soviet puppet government. Developing this sort of unity is not easy.

Czechoslovak leaders made unwise concessions in Moscow. In retrospect, they should not have made any agreements except after consultation with the people.

It should also be noted that Soviet government was unprepared to deal with a nonviolent resistance. Perhaps there were more subtle ways of imposing its mandates, without an invasion.

In summary, important lessons from Czechoslovakia 1968 are (1) remaining nonviolent is crucial; (2) resistance organised by the people is stronger than resistance directed by the government; (3) fraternisation is a powerful technique; (4) resilient communication systems providing accurate information are vital; (5) maintaining unity of the resistance is vital; (6) leaders need to understand the dynamics of nonviolent resistance.

Soviet Union, 1991[42]

The Soviet Union was formed as a result of the 1917 Russian revolution, which overthrew the Kerensky government (which had earlier toppled the regime of the autocratic Czar) and replaced it with a state socialist government. Before long it became a socialist dictatorship under Josef Stalin. During World War II, the Soviet Union was allied with Britain and the US against Nazi Germany, and afterwards the Soviet government installed puppet governments in several eastern European states, including Poland, East Germany, Hungary and Czechoslovakia.

In 1989, while Mikhail Gorbachev was leader of the Soviet Union, there was a peaceful challenge to the governments of eastern European countries, which became independent and switched from state socialism to capitalism and representative government. In the Soviet Union, Gorbachev's liberal policies and the loss of the eastern European empire were unwelcome to adherents of old-style Soviet approaches.

On 19 August 1991, there was a coup. Gorbachev was arrested at his dacha in the Crimea. All military units were put on alert. Tanks were sent to Moscow, Leningrad and other cities, and plans were made for mass arrests. Strikes and rallies were banned, liberal newspapers were closed and broadcast media were controlled, so most of the country had no news of resistance.

---

42 Monica Attard, *Russia: Which Way Paradise?* (Sydney: Doubleday, 1997); Victoria E. Bonnell, Ann Cooper, and Gregory Freidin (eds.), *Russia at the Barricades: Eyewitness Accounts of the August 1991 Coup* (Armonk, NY: M. E. Sharpe, 1994); Jeremy Gambrell, "Seven days that shook the world," *New York Review of Books,* Vol. 38, No. 15, 26 September 1991, pp. 56–61; Brian Martin and Wendy Varney, *Nonviolence Speaks: Communicating Against Repression* (Cresskill, NJ: Hampton Press, 2003), pp. 46–57; Vladimir Pozner, *Eyewitness: A Personal Account of the Unraveling of the Soviet Union* (New York: Random House, 1992); Martin Sixsmith, *Moscow Coup: The Death of the Soviet System* (London: Simon & Schuster, 1991).

This was not so much a military coup as a political coup to reintroduce authoritarian state socialism. The coup leaders seemed to have all the advantages: backing from the armed forces, the KGB (Soviet secret police), the Communist Party and the police, plus the Soviet people's long acceptance of authority.

The news said Gorbachev was ill and an emergency committee had taken over. Most listeners immediately assumed there had been a coup, a conclusion reinforced when they saw tanks in the streets. The first sign of resistance was the tone of disgust in the voices of newsreaders.

There was an immediate response, including protests, strikes and messages of opposition. Across the country, including at major industrial complexes, many workers went on strike or just stayed home.

Some civilians stood in the path of tanks, whose drivers then took another route. Rallies were held; when the army did not disperse the crowd, this provided a boost for the demonstrators. Commanders had to decide between attacking – and causing casualties – and standing aside. The protests caused an internal debate among the plotters.

Moscow journalists from prohibited newspapers worked long hours producing one-page illegal editions in the style of dissident writing, then posted them around the city. In a television broadcast, interviewers asked tough questions of coup leaders. The camera zoomed in on the trembling fingers of coup leader Gennadi Yanayev, leading to jokes around the country. Many citizens still had short-wave radios and pulled them out of storage to use as independent channels of communication.

In several cities, makeshift systems were developed to collect information and coordinate resistance. In Leningrad, for example, taxi drivers drove around looking for evidence of troop movements so they could alert demonstrators. The drivers used their taxi radios to coordinate their efforts.

Talking to troops was important, including pleas, persuasion and jokes. Protesters also shared sweets and cigarettes with soldiers. A foreign journalist asked a tank commander whether he would fire on protesters if ordered to. The commander thought a bit and replied, "You know, I'm Russian, just like all of them. I think I'd rather go to jail for treason than shoot at my own people."[43]

---

43 Attard, *Russia,* 182–183.

Political figure Boris Yeltsin became the symbolic leader of the resistance, operating from the Russian White House in Moscow where a small short-wave broadcasting studio was set up. Yeltsin's optimistic claims about resistance helped trigger actual resistance. After his message, tanks then left (perhaps by coincidence), providing a psychological victory for the resistance.

The coup leaders instructed a special forces unit, the KGB's Alpha Team, to capture the White House. The commander of the team, Victor Karpukhin, claimed he was in charge of arresting Yeltsin and boasted, "I did everything I could to do nothing."[44]

During this time, western governments did nothing practical to support the resistance. US President George Bush initially gave encouragement for the coup but then opposed it when it seemed to be weakening. The Soviet people had to rely on their own efforts, and they succeeded. Within a few days the coup collapsed, almost entirely due to popular noncooperation.

---

44 Peter Reddaway and Dmitri Glinski, *The Tragedy of Russia's Reforms: Market Bolshevism against Democracy* (Washington, DC: United States Institute of Peace Press, 2001), p. 205.

Conclusion

Because no society has ever systematically prepared for social defence, there are no precedents for how it might work in practice. Nevertheless, it is possible to learn from historical examples of spontaneous nonviolent resistance to invasions and coups. This is analogous to the way that professional armies might learn from the experience of spontaneous armed campaigns, in which there is little or no preparation, no production or purchase of weapons, and no required training. By looking at spontaneous *un*armed struggles, it is possible to gain insights into the areas of effectiveness and areas needing improvement.

We described two instances of spontaneous nonviolent resistance to invasion and occupation (Czechoslovakia 1968 and Germany 1923) and three instances of spontaneous resistance to coups (Germany 1920, Algeria 1961 and Soviet Union 1991). Several themes emerge. One is the importance of the resistance being unified, including nearly all the civilian population. Another is how nonviolent resistance can lead to noncooperation by some of the troops. Czechoslovak efforts at fraternising with invading troops made some of them "unreliable." In Algeria, soldiers noncooperated by remaining in their barracks and some pilots flew their aircraft away so they could not be used for attack. In the Soviet Union, special forces disobeyed orders to attack the Russian White House. These examples indicate that it is vital to figure out ways to encourage members of the attacking force to rethink their roles and possibly to shirk or disobey orders.

Remaining nonviolent is crucial. This reduces the personal threat to the soldiers and undermines their willingness to use force. In each of the examples, the resistance had the most impact by remaining nonviolent.

Several of the examples show the importance of communication. In Czechoslovakia, the radio network encouraged and coordinated resistance. In Algeria, the broadcast of de Gaulle's call for resistance was important. In the Soviet Union, email was helpful to coup opponents. Resisters need to be ready and able to use various communication channels to express their opposition, to encourage people to resist and to communicate with attackers.

In each of the cases we selected, the nonviolent resistance was successful at some level. The three coups were defeated. Resistance in the Ruhr had to be terminated, but it helped enable the subsequent withdrawal of French troops. The Czechoslovak resistance was overcome, but the Soviet military victory was accompanied with massive damage to the reputation of the Soviet Union and Communism more generally. In each of the examples of coups, the resistance started immediately, before the coup leaders could cement their positions.

These five cases do not prove that social defence can be effective, but they do provide suggestive ideas about what might be possible. The aim of studying such examples is to learn from the past in order to help create a different future.

4
Ideas about social defence

Social defence, as a concept, is a century old. Since then, many further ideas about it have been proposed and debated. In this chapter, we outline important ideas concerning social defence. For this, we draw on both actions and writings, inspired by nonviolent actions and by analyses of military systems and alternatives to them.

This is not a comprehensive history of social defence ideas. Instead, we highlight a number of key points and give citations to some relevant sources. A full history – which remains to be written – would give credit to both prominent and less known contributions. In "Further reading," we list some significant writings about social defence. This is far from comprehensive, in part because there are important works in languages we cannot read.

Key ideas:

- Social defence is possible.
- Social defence is defence of society or community, not necessarily of territory.
- Social defence can challenge the state monopoly over legitimate violence.
- Social defence can be organised hierarchically or via networks.
- Social defence can be introduced by governments or through social movements.
- Armed resistance is usually detrimental to nonviolent resistance.
- Planning and training are crucial to social defence.
- Social defence should be organised around defending the centre of gravity.
- Communication systems are crucial to social defence.
- Dealing with propaganda and disinformation is vital.
- Information about threats should be collected and analysed.
- A key focus for persuasion is the armed forces of the aggressor.
- Skill development is crucial.
- Technological systems should be designed for social defence.
- Transitioning to social defence is a social change process.

- Many different social movements have affinities with social defence.
- Experience in nonviolent action is an effective preparation for social defence.
- Social defence can be accompanied by social attack.
- Nonviolent action has four dimensions relevant to social defence.

Social defence is possible

The idea of defending without violence is a challenge to conventional ways of thinking. This idea is fairly new, and not well known.

As noted in chapter 1, during the Great War (World War I), British philosopher Bertrand Russell proposed defending the country by citizen action rather than armed force.[45] Since then, many others have proposed this idea and elaborated on it.

The basic idea is important, but it is not obvious. The usual assumption is that the only way to defend against aggression is by armed force. Most people today assume this. Indeed, to defend without violence seems almost crazy. People are familiar with wars from the history books, Hollywood films and the news. They seldom hear about nonviolent alternatives, so the assumption persists that defence means military defence.

The inspiration for early proponents of social defence was successful unarmed resistance in several historical episodes, notably Hungarians against the Austrian empire in the mid 1800s and Finns against Russian domination in 1898–1905.[46] If people could resist oppressive domination without arms, it is a short conceptual step to think they could resist military invasion and that this could be a replacement for military systems. This might seem straightforward but is not obvious, for two reasons. First, historical episodes of nonviolent resistance are not nearly so well known as wars and military operations. Second, the idea of nonviolent resistance, required to understand the historical episodes, is itself quite new. Indeed, the birth of nonviolence

---

45 Bertrand Russell, "War and non-resistance," *Atlantic Monthly,* 116, August 1915, pp. 266–274.

46 Tamás Csapody and Thomas Weber, "Hungarian nonviolent resistance against Austria and its place in the history of nonviolence," *Peace & Change,* 32, 4, 2007, pp. 499–519; Steven Duncan Huxley, *Constitutionalist Insurgency in Finland: Finnish "Passive Resistance" against Russification as a Case of Nonmilitary Struggle in the European Resistance Tradition* (Helsinki: Finnish Historical Society, 1990).

as a strategy of resistance is often taken as 11 September 1906 when, at a meeting in South Africa addressed by Gandhi, thousands of Indians pledged to resist an oppressive ordinance.

Social defence is defence of society or community, not necessarily of territory

Military forces are most commonly thought of as defending territories. The borders between countries are seen as defining separate entities that must be protected from invaders, and sometimes from immigrants. This idea of nations, territories and borders is dominant today, so much so that it is hard to imagine anything different. Travelling requires going through borders, which are often patrolled. Passports are inspected. In this context, it seems natural that defence is assumed to be defence of a home territory. (We can set aside for the moment the reality that in many cases military systems oppress the population within borders.)

Much of the writing about social defence assumes it is a functional replacement for military defence and therefore involves defending a nation, with its usual borders. It is thought of as national defence. However, a number of commentators have emphasised that the key thing that should be defended is society or community. This means defending the practices and institutions that enable people to live cooperatively. This can include political practices such as free speech and assembly, economic practices such as production and distribution of goods and services, and social practices such as care for children.

As described in chapter 1, British war veteran and commentator Stephen King-Hall argued that defence should be defence of a way of life.[47] He took the way of life to be defended to be British parliamentary democracy in the 1950s. Many people might see other models as more desirable. The point is that what is to be defended is not a territory but a social system, and the positive values underlying it.

Focusing on values to be defended – for example, respect for life, inclusiveness and supporting those in need – can reduce the tendency to demonise potential enemies. When social defence is *for* positive values, there is less likelihood of fear and hatred.

---

47 Stephen King-Hall, *Defence in the Nuclear Age* (London: Victor Gollancz, 1958).

Social defence challenges the state monopoly over legitimate violence

Many writers have assumed the goal of a social defence system is to defend a country against external aggression, which means defence of the state. The state here refers to the government and various associated entities, with sovereignty over a territory. However, it is possible to drop the assumption that social defence involves defending a state and instead think of it as defending a community, which may not have a formal government.

Max Weber, the pioneering sociologist, famously defined the state as the entity claiming a monopoly over organised violence within a territory. Organised violence means the police and the military, which are used to defend against internal and external enemies, including any challenges to the state itself. But what does a monopoly over organised violence mean when the military is dissolved and replaced by a mobilised, unarmed citizenry? The implication is that the state is no longer defined by its capacity for violence. Therefore, what does it mean to defend the state without using violence? With a national social defence system, the state might be redefined as the entity having popular support within a community against enemies. In any case, the role of the state becomes questionable if there is no capacity for organised violence.

This is especially important given that social defence is protection against state violence. If a community is organised to nonviolently resist aggression and oppression, this capacity can be used against the state. Social defence is protection against coups of all sorts.

Social defence can be organised hierarchically or via networks

Militaries are usually organised hierarchically. Troops have commanders and the commanders have superiors and so on up to the commander-in-chief. The hierarchy is manifest in military ranks, such as private, corporal and general.

One model for social defence is a similar hierarchy, perhaps not so formal, but still run from the top. The defence system would have a commander or leadership team that would set the direction for resistance, make calls for actions and determine strategic priorities. Various groups, for example workers in particular industries, churches and government agencies, would each have their roles to play, and each would be led by a single leader or a leadership group, just as they are now.

The hierarchical model has definite advantages. It ensures coordinated action in service of an overall aim, preventing contradictory or counterproductive actions by segments of the resistance. However, it also has disadvantages. The aggressor might target the leadership, for example by kidnapping and threatening to torture family members, or just by imprisoning or killing the key leaders. Alternatively, the aggressor might buy off the leadership through offers of jobs or other opportunities. Finally, too much power at the top can be corrupting: leaders may seek to entrench their own positions and privileges.[48]

Another model for social defence is based on networks. Various groups would be prepared to resist and to take action autonomously, without a central command. Groups would communicate with each other about plans, preparations, successes and failures. Coordinated action could occur if multiple groups decided to join an initiative.

In this model, leadership remains important, but it must be a sort of leadership that is inclusive and consultative, rather than top-down. In a study of communities that were able to stay out of wars, this sort of leadership was vital: "Leadership styles were inclusive, nonhierarchical, communicative, responsive, receptive, and respectful. Many leaders claimed that, rather than leading, they were themselves being led by the broader community.

---

48 David Kipnis, *The Powerholders* (Chicago: University of Chicago Press, 1976); *Technology and Power* (New York: Springer-Verlag, 1990); Ian Robertson, *The Winner Effect: How Power Affects Your Brain* (London: Bloomsbury, 2012).

Leadership was embedded in the communities, and the communities selected and needed their leadership. Leaders were accessible, listening, consultative, and accountable."[49]

An advantage of network-based defence is that it enables local initiative and learning from what works and what doesn't.[50] It is especially relevant when repression is harsh so that resistance leaders are removed from the scene. On the other hand, relying on networks may make it difficult to mobilise large actions, and leave out parts of the population that are not connected to networks.

Social defence can be introduced by governments or through social movements

When defence using nonviolent methods is seen as national defence, directly replacing the functions of military defence, it seems plausible to encourage governments to introduce it. This has been attempted for many decades. Advocates of civilian-based defence have argued that it would be more effective than military defence. As well, they argue that civilian-based defence would reduce the risk of foreign invasion: having no military eliminates the threat to potential invaders and the rationale for pre-emptive war.

Few governments have been receptive to these arguments. There have been a few investigations, for example in the Netherlands.[51] In Sweden, social defence is one component of national defence, along with military defence, civil defence and psychological defence – but in this case social defence is subordinated to military defence and there is no training or preparation for civilians.

In the United States, pre-eminent nonviolence researcher Gene Sharp tried to interest the military in civilian-based defence. A few individuals became interested, but overall Sharp's efforts had little impact. This is in contrast with his massive influence on nonviolent activism worldwide.

---

49 Mary B. Anderson and Marshall Wallace, *Opting Out of War: Strategies to Prevent Violent Conflict* (Boulder, CO: Lynne Rienner, 2013), pp. 57–58.

50 For an informative discussion of how activists varied their tactics according to local circumstances, see Janjira Sombatpoonsiri, *Humor and Nonviolent Struggle in Serbia* (US: Syracuse University Press, 2015).

51 Giliam de Valk in cooperation with Johan Niezing, *Research on Civilian-Based Defence* (Amsterdam: SISWO, 1993) reports numerous possible projects, but only one was funded.

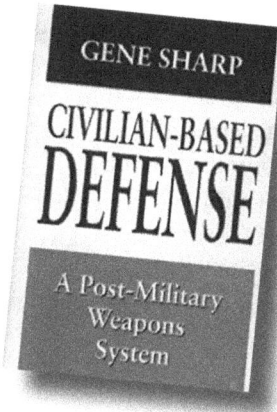

Sharp believed that his concept of civilian-based defence was so superior to military means that he would be able to convince generals and governments to change. The Lithuanian defence minister declared, after reading Sharp's book *Civilian-Based Defense*,[52] "I would rather have this book than the atomic bomb." Inspired by such reactions, Sharp worked hard to get access to decision makers in a number of countries but, despite some positive initial responses, none took the ideas seriously enough to implement them.[53]

Rather than try to convince governments to introduce social defence, an alternative path is to raise the idea in social movements and to encourage them to incorporate elements contributing to social defence in their thinking and campaigning.[54] The peace movement is the most obvious candidate to promote social defence measures, though it has mainly campaigned against war rather than building capacity for nonviolent action. The environmental movement, by promoting local self-sufficiency in renewable energy production, makes communities less vulnerable to hostile takeover. The labour movement is crucial: when workers have the understanding and skills to take over workplaces and operations, they are ideally placed to resist aggressors. This includes workers in factories, farms and offices. Government employees can play a potent role by refusing to cooperate with occupiers, so administering government operations becomes impossible.

In the 1980s, various groups in several different countries sought to promote social defence through movements.[55] However, after the end of

---

52 Gene Sharp with Bruce Jenkins, *Civilian-Based Defense: A Post-Military Weapons System* (Princeton, NJ: Princeton University Press, 1990).

53 Robert J. Burrowes, *The Strategy of Nonviolent Defense: A Gandhian Perspective* (Albany, NY: State University of New York Press, 1996), pp. 154–162, is strongly critical of Sharp's approach. He calls it "civilian-based defence," contrasting it with "social defence," a grassroots perspective. We also favour the grassroots perspective but are not so worried about the label.

54 Brian Martin, *Social Defence, Social Change* (London: Freedom Press, 1993).

55 The history of grassroots activism to promote social defence remains to be written.

the Cold War, most of this effort ceased. Nevertheless, even though social defence is seldom on the formal agenda of social movements, many of their campaigning efforts are helping strengthen the capacity of communities to resist aggression.[56]

This book is oriented to the promotion of social defence through grassroots efforts. We do not expect to convince governments. In fact, governments are one of the least likely groups to promote social defence, because a population empowered to use nonviolent action can turn their skills against the government itself. A corollary is that the more repressive the government, the less interest it is likely to have in social defence and hence the greater the priority there should be on promoting it through social movements.

Armed resistance is usually detrimental to nonviolent resistance

There is much research showing that protests are more effective when the protesters do not use violence against the police or others. This is called maintaining nonviolent discipline. If police or soldiers attack peaceful protesters, many observers see this as unjustified and their sympathies can shift in favour of the protesters. In some instances, this shift is so strong that protesters receive a surge of support, a process called political jiu-jitsu.[57]

When some protesters use violence, for example hitting police or throwing bricks at them, this undermines nonviolent discipline. The confrontation is then seen by many observers as one involving violence on both sides, even when most of the violence is by the police. The prospects for political jiu-jitsu are reduced.

For this reason, in some documented cases police agents have pretended to be protesters and encouraged violence, or even initiated it.[58] By doing this,

---

56 For more on this, see chapter 6.

57 Gene Sharp, *The Politics of Nonviolent Action* (Boston: Porter Sargent, 1973), pp. 657–703. See also "Backfire materials," http://www.bmartin.cc/pubs/backfire.html.

58 Many experienced activists can tell stories about agents provocateurs. On the spying dimension, see Eveline Lubbers, *Secret Manoeuvres in the Dark: Corporate and Police Spying on Activists* (London: Pluto Press, 2012). For the perspective of agencies opposing social movements, see Eric L. Nelson, "Subversion of social movements by adversarial agents," *International Journal of Intelligence and CounterIntelligence*, vol.

they hope to discredit the protesters. There is no known case in which police infiltrators have encouraged nonviolent discipline.

Social defence is basically the application of methods of nonviolent action to the purpose of defending a community against aggression. Therefore, incorporating armed methods of resistance in a social defence struggle is likely to undermine its effectiveness.[59]

Planning and training are crucial to social defence

As noted in chapter 3, the historical examples of nonviolent resistance to invasions – Germany 1923 and Czechoslovakia 1968 – were spontaneous. There was no preparation for unarmed resistance prior to the occupations. Yet the resistance in each case was remarkably successful, all things considered.

Spontaneous nonviolent resistance is analogous to spontaneous armed resistance: it has a chance of success, but not nearly as much chance as when resistance is carefully planned.

Militaries undertake extensive planning and training. They analyse possible threats and prepare contingency plans. They plan their requirements for equipment. They buy or develop weapons systems. They run extensive training programmes for their troops. They have troops practise using their weapons. They run "exercises" to simulate battles. Without training and specially designed equipment, militaries would be much less potent.

Studies of US troops on the front lines in the landings on Normandy during World War II showed that only one quarter of them fired their rifles, an indication that most men are reluctant to kill other men. Since then, US training has drawn on psychological research to improve shooting rates, which reached 90% during the Vietnam war.[60] Psychological research has also been used to determine optimal ways for soldiers to bond into a fighting unit.

26, 2013, pp. 161–175.

59 Erica Chenoweth and Kurt Schock, "Do contemporaneous armed challenges affect the outcomes of mass nonviolent campaigns?" *Mobilization*, vol. 20, no. 4, 2015, pp. 427–451: "… we can argue with some confidence that on average, maximalist nonviolent campaigns often succeed *despite* violent flanks – rarely because of them" (p. 447). In other words, armed resistance usually hurts rather than helps nonviolent movements.

60 Dave Grossman, *On Killing: The Psychological Cost of Learning to Kill in War and Society* (Boston: Little, Brown, 1995).

Admittedly, militaries are notorious for wasteful spending, rigid rules that inhibit initiative, dysfunctional hierarchies and unwillingness to learn from mistakes. Nevertheless, military operations have become far more effective over the years due to massive investments in infrastructure, equipment, training, logistics and strategic analysis.

Compared to this, most armed uprisings are amateurish, with little training and limited weaponry. This is a key reason why armed challenge to a well prepared military is nearly always futile.

Similarly, unarmed resistance to aggression can be made far more effective by extensive planning and preparation. The parallel to training of soldiers is training of citizens in methods of resistance. This might include regular sessions over many years, including simulations of rallies, boycotts, strikes and fraternisation. Planning would include careful analyses of possible threats. Preparation would include building of links with citizen resisters in other parts of the world, learning of foreign languages, and application of insights from the psychology of nonviolent struggle.

It is fair to say that there has been hardly any preparation and training for social defence. There is much to learn about what this might involve.

Social defence should be organised around defending the centre of gravity

Carl von Clausewitz was a German military strategist who wrote the book *On War,* published in 1832. This book is now considered a classic, and many of its ideas are considered relevant to military strategy today.[61]

Anders Boserup and Andrew Mack wrote an important book about social defence, *War without Weapons,* published in 1974.[62] One of their insights was that social defence is analogous to guerrilla warfare rather than to conventional military operations. Guerrilla warfare is a form of people's warfare, with popular support for resistance to a foe having superior weaponry and resources. Social defence is similar except that violence is not used.

One of Clausewitz's important concepts is the "centre of gravity." This refers to the key aspect of an armed struggle that must be protected for the effort to continue. If the enemy can destroy the centre of gravity, then it can

---

61 Carl von Clausewitz. *Vom Kriege* (Berlin: Ferdinand Dümmler, 1832).

62 Anders Boserup and Andrew Mack, *War Without Weapons: Non-violence in National Defence* (London: Frances Pinter, 1974).

succeed. Likewise, destroying the enemy's centre of gravity means defeating the enemy.

Boserup and Mack applied Clausewitz's concept of the centre of gravity to social defence. Their assessment is that the centre of gravity is the *unity* of the resistance. Unity here refers to the commitment of different sectors of the society defending against aggression. As long as all the sectors – workers and managers, urban and rural, men and women, liberals and conservatives – remain committed to resistance, then it can maintain the struggle. However, if some sectors defect or give up, then the nonviolent resistance can be defeated. When societies are divided, with contending groups each claiming to represent the public interest, they are much more vulnerable to external aggression and civil war.

Gene Keyes, a nonviolence researcher, looked at the Danish nonviolent resistance to the Nazi occupation.[63] He also looked at the centre of gravity, and came to a different assessment than Boserup and Mack. Keyes said the centre of gravity is the *morale* of the resistance. Even without unity, as long as resisters believe they can succeed, the resistance can continue.

Robert Burrowes, a nonviolent activist and scholar, wrote *The Strategy of Nonviolent Defense: A Gandhian Perspective*. Burrowes also looked at the centre of gravity and came up with yet a different view. He included two components in the centre of gravity of nonviolent defence: the power and will of the resistance. According to Burrowes, the strategic aim of the defence should be to "to consolidate the power and will of the defending population to resist the aggression." Burrowes also looked at the centre of gravity of the opponent, namely the aggressor, and identified the same factors, power and will. The strategic aim of the counteroffensive becomes "to *alter* the will of the opponent elite to conduct the aggression, and to *undermine* their power to do so." So for Burrowes, the key consideration in planning a social

---

63 Gene Keyes, "Strategic non-violent defense: the construct of an option," *Journal of Strategic Studies,* vol. 4, no. 2, June 1981, pp. 125–151.

defence system is how to maintain the power and will of the defenders while targeting the power and will of the aggressor.[64]

Boserup and Mack, Keyes and Burrowes reach different conclusions about the centre of gravity, the key element that should guide the conduct of social defence. It could be the unity of the resistance, the morale of the resistance, or the power and will of the resistance. These three conceptions are not dramatically different: they all involve psychology, in particular some form of commitment. Unity involves commitment to struggle and to others in the struggle. Morale involves commitment to continuing the struggle. Will likewise involves commitment.

It may not be possible to resolve the differences without more experience with social defence. In any case, it is bound to be worthwhile to explore ways to promote the unity, morale, and power and will of defenders.

Communication systems are crucial to social defence

Several types of communication are important in nonviolent resistance. One is communication between resisters and opponents. In some historical cases,[65] resisters have talked with soldiers, explained their reasons for protesting, countered misinformation and developed personal connections. This technique is called fraternisation. It can weaken the soldiers' resolve and sometimes lead them to disobey orders. Fraternisation operates best in one-on-one conversations or other face-to-face interactions. This does not happen automatically, and it can be facilitated by communication systems.[66]

---

64 Robert J. Burrowes, *The Strategy of Nonviolent Defense: A Gandhian Perspective* (Albany, NY: State University of New York Press, 1996), p. 209.

65 See chapter 3 for examples.

66 For an excellent analysis of fraternisation strategies, see Anika Locke Binnendijk and Ivan Marovic, "Power and persuasion: nonviolent strategies to influence state security forces in Serbia (2000) and Ukraine (2004)," *Communist and Post-Communist Studies*, vol. 39, no. 3, September 2006, pp. 411–429.

Mechanised opponents, such as drones and robots, are a different matter. Will machines become so intelligent that it would be possible to develop relationships with them and encourage them to withdraw or change sides? If not, then fraternising would have to be done upstream, with those who design and deploy fighting machines.

A second important type of communication is between resisters and other members of the population. In most struggles, a relatively small percentage of the population is publicly active, for example participating in rallies. A far greater number of people can participate in boycotts and strikes. To make these methods work well, communication is needed between resistance leaders and the wider population, to win people over and inform them of activities. Alternatively, in a more decentralised resistance, members of the population need to know what is happening so they can be inspired and join in.

A third important type of communication is between active resisters, for example participants in a protest. Coordination is needed and decisions need to be made, and these require reliable communication systems.

Decades ago, ensuring secure communication systems was more difficult. In a military coup, for example, usurpers would take over radio and television facilities and there would be no easy means for resisters to get their message to the wider public. Today, with the proliferation of social media, resistance communication seems easier: just use smartphones. But what if the mobile network is shut down? What if opponents use surveillance techniques to track down resistance leaders and torture their families? What if attackers use bots to disseminate misleading information or to swamp channels with millions of fake messages?[67]

The key in all these situations is preparation. This means designing communication systems so that resisters find them easy to use and secure against disruption and surveillance. It also means ensuring that people have the knowledge and skills to use communication systems well, for example to set up emergency channels, counter disinformation and craft persuasive messages.

---

67 See, for example, Brian Martin and Wendy Varney, *Nonviolence Speaks: Communicating against Repression* (Cresskill, NJ: Hampton Press, 2003); Zeynep Tufekci, *Twitter and Tear Gas: The Power and Fragility of Networked Protest* (New Haven, CT: Yale University Press, 2017).

Dealing with propaganda and disinformation is vital

In some wars, everyone knows who is on each side. In the war between Japan and the United States 1941–1945, each side used propaganda, but mainly to build support from within their own country. Japanese propaganda had little influence in the US and US propaganda had little influence in Japan.

However, in many wars, especially civil wars, the struggle for loyalties is crucial. One or both sides may produce leaflets, posters, graffiti, television advertisements, and social media commentary intended to sway opinions. There can also be disinformation: intentionally false or misleading information with a political goal, for example to discredit the opponent. Disinformation could include claims about vices of political leaders, the state of the economy, the actions of foreign governments, or dissent within the population.

In some nonviolent struggles against aggression, propaganda is not so important. For example, when Soviet troops invaded Czechoslovakia in 1968, the spontaneous nonviolent resistance was unified. The main disinformation was the Soviet government telling its own troops that they were being sent to Czechoslovakia to stop a capitalist takeover.

However, in many struggles the role of propaganda and disinformation is much more important, and this is likely to be the case with a social defence system. An aggressor might claim to be bringing democracy, defending against terrorism or tackling corruption. This is even more likely when the aggression is internal, namely when there is an armed takeover or insurrection.

For a social defence system to be effective, there needs to be a well developed capacity for dealing with propaganda and disinformation. It

would be useful for there to be analysts or commentators who expose these techniques and who have credibility. There could be educational materials on how to detect and expose propaganda, and people could learn about the psychology of belief. More generally, it would be helpful for people to have a better understanding of how society operates so they can easily recognise false and misleading claims.

Writings on social defence have not devoted much attention to propaganda. When writers assume social defence is organised by the government, then it is easy to assume that the population will mobilise behind the government and against aggressors. The more complex cases, in which there is a furious or devious struggle for loyalty, have not been dealt with.

A social defence system is not well served by typical relationships with information sources. When people believe the news or do not delve more deeply into how governments, corporations and other groups shape messages (for example concerning terrorism, crime or policing), they are vulnerable to being fed misleading ideas. When people are easily influenced by political promises, they are vulnerable to manipulation. Skills and practice are needed for resisting propaganda and disinformation.

Imagine a group of people getting together to learn how to recognise and counter propaganda. They could learn about what makes information reliable, how emotions are triggered by words and images, and how to discover who is promoting messages. As part of their study, the group could be tested by being given slogans, articles or posters and asked to determine what techniques are being used to persuade the audience and whether these are manipulative. The group might also prepare its own propaganda messages in order to learn how this is done, and compare its assessments of messages with those made by other study groups.

Learning about propaganda is possible today. It is not common, though, perhaps in part because governments and advertisers use these techniques every day and do not want to encourage critical examination of their methods and messages.

Information about threats should be collected and analysed

In any defence system, it is important to learn about possible threats. In military systems, doing this is called "intelligence" and can involve having spies in other countries, using aircraft or satellites to photograph foreign installations, undertaking surveillance of electronic communications, and analysing publicly available information such as speeches and news reports. Intelligence operations are often carried out in secrecy, and assessments of threats are often available only to selected recipients on a need-to-know basis.

Just like military defence, a social defence system also needs some sort of intelligence operation in order to assess likely threats and to prepare accordingly. If there is a possibility of an invasion from a foreign country, then it is important to know about the potential invader's preparations and plans. Information can be collected in various ways, for example by studying foreign news reports and talking to citizens and soldiers in the foreign country.

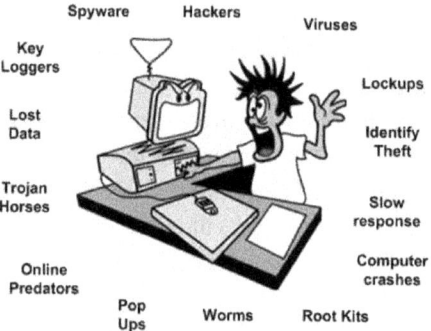

Threats can also arise internally. There might be a group planning some sort of takeover using violence. So there should be ways to collect information about plots and hostile preparations.

The next question is how to make use of the information obtained. The usual sorts of intelligence operations are secret, but this means that there is a risk that insiders will abuse their power or that enemy operatives will infiltrate agencies. An alternative is "publicly shared intelligence."[68] An agency would seek information, make assessments and publish the assessments for everyone to see. Members of the public could then examine the assessments and send in new information, point to mistakes in the information and identify flaws in the analysis.

---

68 Giliam de Valk and Brian Martin, "Publicly shared intelligence," *First Monday: Peer-reviewed Journal on the Internet,* vol. 11, no. 9, 2006.

In the 1980s, South Africa was still ruled under the racist system of apartheid that oppressed the majority black population. The United Nations imposed economic sanctions on the country. An important part of the sanctions was a ban on supplying oil, but some shipping companies broke the sanctions in their quest for profits. In the Netherlands, there was a non-government organisation called the Shipping Research Bureau that collected information about ships that broke the sanctions. The Bureau solicited information from anyone, and had anonymous sources within some of the companies. (These would today be called leakers.)

Importantly, the Bureau published its assessments, identifying companies that were breaking sanctions. Occasionally it made mistakes, which were pointed out by informed individuals, enabling the Bureau to make improvements. Because its assessments were public, they became much more accurate – more accurate than those of the Dutch government intelligence agencies.

In a social defence system, there might be several agencies producing publicly shared intelligence, competing with each other to produce the most accurate and useful assessments. People would then have more confidence in the assessments, and could feed in their own information. Social defence is a people's defence system, so it makes sense that its intelligence operations should also take maximum advantage of information and insights from the entire population.

A key focus for persuasion is the armed forces of the aggressor

In wars, the soldiers on each side are a threat to each other, and this helps to build loyalty on each side: the opponents are the enemy, and helping the enemy is traitorous.

However, with social defence, there are soldiers on one side and civilians on the other side. The civilians pose no physical threat to the soldiers. This makes it more difficult for many of the soldiers to use force against the population. It is quite different from an enemy that shoots back. By its very nature, namely being nonviolent, social defence can undermine the loyalty or commitment of the aggressor's armed forces.

In addition, there is the technique of fraternisation: talking with soldiers to convince them to refuse to join in aggressive or repressive actions.[69]

Persuading opponent soldiers is an important factor to consider when choosing resistance actions. Strikes and boycotts usually have no direct impact on soldiers. A different sort of technique is social ostracism; applied to soldiers, this involves refusing to serve or even talk with them. This is a powerful method, but it needs to be balanced against the value of trying to be friends with soldiers in order to win them over.

It is likely to be counter-productive to shout abuse at soldiers. This is not physically violent but nevertheless can cause them to become more hostile. The key is to treat them as potential allies and choose tactics that contribute to this possibility.[70]

Skill development is crucial

Soldiers spend considerable time – months or years – training in order to become good at their jobs. Social defenders, to be really effective, should be spending an equivalent time and effort to develop their skills.

---

69   This was discussed earlier in relation to communication systems. On the importance of fraternisation in revolutions, see Katherine Chorley, *Armies and the Art of Revolution* (London: Faber and Faber, 1943); Sharon Erickson Nepstad, *Nonviolent Revolutions: Civil Resistance in the Late 20th Century* (Oxford: Oxford University Press, 2011). Studies of communities that avoided war show the importance of talking with fighters: "Far from staying below the radar, nonwar communities established relations with fighting groups and negotiated with them. Through a proactive approach, they forced combatants to talk to them and thus recognize their nonwarring status." Mary B. Anderson and Marshall Wallace, *Opting Out of War: Strategies to Prevent Violent Conflict* (Boulder, CO: Lynne Rienner, 2013), p. 69.

70   By far the most useful discussion of psychology relevant to loyalty and fraternisation is Rachel MacNair, "The psychology of agents of repression: the paradox of defection," in Lester R. Kurtz and Lee A. Smithey (eds.), *The Paradox of Repression and Nonviolent Movements* (Syracuse, NY: Syracuse University Press, 2018), pp. 74–101. See also Samantha Reis and Brian Martin, "Psychological dynamics of outrage against injustice," *Peace Research: The Canadian Journal of Peace and Conflict Studies*, vol. 40, no. 1, 2008, pp. 5–23.

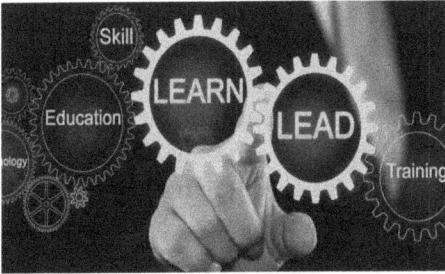

Research on expert performance looks at what is required to develop highly advanced skills in swimming, playing chess, playing the piano and all sorts of other areas.[71] What is needed is continual practice, under the guidance of a good teacher, targeted at improving in the weakest areas of the specific task, for example playing a difficult musical passage over and over, slower and faster, until it is mastered, and then moving onto a more difficult passage. This is called "deliberate practice." It is not the same as using the skill. A pianist might play several hours at a nightclub every evening, but this is exercising the skill of performing, not practising it. A pianist who spends an hour per day in private practice, with regular sessions with an experienced teacher, will improve more than the nightclub pianist.

To become a world-class performer in any field – as a writer, speaker, athlete or strategist – requires thousands of hours of deliberate practice. This sort of practice is hard work, requiring intense concentration, so usually the most practice that anyone can do is about four hours per day. This means that acquiring world-class skills takes years, usually quite a few years.

For those not seeking such advanced skills, the same principles apply: deliberate practice is the best way to improve. A few hundred hours of such practice, or just a few dozen, can build considerable skills.[72]

An important requirement for development of skills is good teachers or guidance. This is to ensure that the right approach is taken, to provide feedback on performance and to refine capabilities. As individuals improve, often they can adequately monitor their own performance, though guidance is still useful.

In many fields, insights from research on expert performance are seldom applied. For example, teachers and doctors, after their initial training, mainly use their skills rather than practise them with a focus on improvement. Few

71 Anders Ericsson and Robert Pool, *Peak: Secrets from the New Science of Expertise* (London: Bodley Head, 2016).

72 For what is possible in a shorter period, see Josh Kaufman, *The First 20 Hours: How to Learn Anything … **Fast*** (New York: Penguin, 2014).

teachers spend even an hour per day practising their skills in communication or subject design. In business, workers mainly do the job, spending little time practising it.

The same applies to nonviolent action. Protesters might attend a few workshops, but few of them regularly practise relevant skills.[73]

For an effective social defence system, insights from research on expert performance would be applied systematically. Skills needed for defending would be identified and practised regularly, with some individuals encouraged to develop advanced skills.

Because fraternisation is crucial, skills in fraternising are especially valuable. The skills involved include being a persuasive communicator, understanding the language and culture of possible aggressors, being able to adapt messages and communication styles to the psychology and circumstances of individuals being talked to, and being able to judge the impact of one's efforts. Even though talking to an invading soldier seems straightforward, there is much to learn and to practise. It is possible to imagine engaging in regular training in groups, in the manner of training in martial arts, as well as fieldwork in the form of trying to persuade local people or foreigners about various matters.

Fraternisation is just one area for skill development. Others include using communication technology, interpreting political developments that might pose a threat, and implementing strategic principles.

Communication skills are also relevant to promoting the idea of social defence, so there is a connection between skill development for defending nonviolently and skill development for promoting social defence.

In a well-developed social defence system, children might learn basic skills and practise them in drills designed as stimulating games, as another sort of sport. For those who are older, there could be specialisation in some relevant skills, as well as regular practice across a range of areas.

A crucial part of practising is having suitably knowledgeable teachers and trainers. Becoming an expert in training others for social defence skills would be an invaluable role.

---

73 Brian Martin and Patrick G. Coy, "Skills, training and activism," *Reflective Practice*, vol. 18, no. 4, 2017, pp. 515–525.

Technological systems should be designed for social defence

The vital functions of energy, transport, agriculture, water supply and factories are examples of "technological systems." They involve equipment and human activities combined into complex systems to deliver services. These systems can be designed to make social defence more effective.[74]

An aggressor can take over vital facilities and use them to subordinate the population. For example, electricity supply is vital in most industrialised societies. If electricity is shut off, or just threatened to be cut off, some people may become more submissive. Therefore, resistance can be aided by technological systems that enable self-reliance or even self-sufficiency.

Local energy systems – relying on rooftop solar, local wind power and microhydro power – are less vulnerable to disruption. An aggressor or terrorist can take over or destroy a large fossil-fuel or nuclear power plant, holding a community to ransom. However, it makes little sense for an aggressor to take over rooftop solar panels or for a terrorist to destroy them. Another way to reduce energy vulnerabilities is through design of buildings and processes. For example, passive solar design can reduce the energy requirements in a building dramatically. So far, solar design has involved balancing energy savings and the extra cost of construction. Social defence offers additional considerations: designing buildings so resisters can make full use of facilities for communication, hiding dissidents, enabling deliveries of food and health services and ensuring disabled access, among other factors.

Other technological systems should also be designed for survival and supporting continued resistance. Aggressors and terrorists can take over

---

74 Brian Martin, *Technology for Nonviolent Struggle* (London: War Resisters' International, 2001).

or destroy major transport nodes, such as airports and rail interchanges. Therefore, if much travel is by foot or bicycle, the disruption is minimised. On the other hand, aggressors might want to use transport systems for their own purposes, for example bringing in military equipment. To support the resistance, transport systems could be designed so that workers, in a crisis, can block movements.

When technological systems are designed to enable a population to be resilient in the face of aggression, this also enables resilience when there are natural disasters such as earthquakes and floods.

It is possible to imagine a scenario in which aggressors threaten to torture or kill workers unless they cooperate. To counter this, some technological systems could be designed so that cooperation is impossible. In a factory, a crucial component could be constructed so that production is halted or slowed, with no quick resumption possible. This might involve a physical piece of equipment for which a replacement is only available in a faraway part of the world, or more easily an encrypted computer component for which the key is inaccessible for a specified time delay.

At a much simpler level, smartphones could be prepared with multiple log-ins. When being forced to log in and provide access to vital information (for example, names of people in the resistance), crisis log-in sequences would automatically delete all sensitive information and provide access only to innocuous or misleading information. This sort of capacity is available already, but few people go to the trouble of preparing for confiscation of their phones. In a social defence system, this sort of preparation would be, by design, made much easier. People would regularly practise how they would behave in a crisis, for example the possibility that the Internet is shut down. This sort of preparation has side benefits. Preparing to resist an aggressor who confiscates your phone is also useful for countering criminals and government spies.

Technological systems are designed by humans for human purposes, including production of food, clothing, shelter, entertainment – and warfare and torture. Social defence involves people preparing to resist aggression and repression without violence, and it only makes sense that technological systems be designed accordingly.

Contemporary militaries are mostly separate from other parts of life: personnel are soldiers, not civilians; weapons systems are largely separate from civilian systems; and daily routines for civilians do not involve much thought about being involved in defence. In contrast, with social defence civilians are on the front line, with everyone potentially involved. This means that civilian technological systems are also defence systems. The implications are far-reaching.

Planning for situations of emergencies must include focus on reducing vulnerabilities of different kinds. A society planning for social defence should build a robust infrastructure and make it possible to function even when sanctions, sabotage, and military occupation are imminent or already present.

The traditional problems with securing shelter, water supply, functioning food chains and acute health service are still high priorities in the new millennium. In addition, modern societies are dependent on a stable electricity grid and a functioning communication system.

For the first list of traditional challenges the general rule is that huge centralised units are more vulnerable than small decentralised ones. Dependence on complex technologies makes the population more exposed to serious problems than systems that can be maintained without specialised expertise. Small scale organic production of food is more robust than gigantic industrialised farming in need of pesticides, huge quantities of fuel, spare parts for advanced machinery and artificial fertilisers. Food production in cities could constitute an important inspiration and building block for a food chain suitable for a future with more secure food production. Big cities in addition need access to land outside the city centre for sufficient production. There are many reasons to eat vegetarian food; one of them is that fewer resources are needed to produce the nutrients needed for a healthy diet.

A resilient society will need both the theoretical knowledge and the practical skills for producing food in this way. It is far from enough to have inspiring books on gardening in your shelves if you do not have the experience of actually growing, tending and harvesting crops. Another important element is to have the capacity to store food after harvesting. For those countries with a climate that does not make it easy to produce all year round, the need for storage is just as important as the production itself. The dominant ways for modern storage are all dependent on electricity. In order to maintain a constant low temperature, refrigerators and freezers are essential. There are alternatives and many of them are possible to use in small scale units. Some of the main alternatives are based on drying the products, fermenting, salting, canning, and cooling in root cellars. Planning for these alternatives should be included in all sectors of our societies, and be integrated in educational systems.

Transitioning to social defence is a social change process

As noted earlier, much writing assumes social defence would be implemented by governments. Military defence is replaced with (or more commonly augmented by) social defence, but other parts of society continue pretty much as before: agriculture, industry, the financial sector and so forth. In this picture, social defence is seen as a functional replacement for military defence: it serves the functions of military defence, only better.

An alternative view – the one we adopt here – is to see the introduction of social defence as a process that also involves massive social change. The experience from decades of advocacy for social defence is that very few governments have any interest in it, and most are hostile. This is easily explained: empowering the people to resist repression means empowering them to be able to resist domination in their own country. This means enabling workers to challenge owners, poor people to challenge exploitation, campaigners to challenge police and students to challenge educational bureaucracies. Within the US government, there has been a degree of support for nonviolent movements opposing repressive rulers – as long as those rulers are in other countries.[75] The US government has done nothing at all to promote nonviolent action by people in the US itself.

If governments do not introduce social defence (or only introduce components of social defence in a controlled way), the alternative is promoting social defence as part of a process of social change. Within workplaces, movements for industrial democracy and workers' control move in the direction needed for workers to develop the skills and capacities to resist repression. In the energy sector, movements for local self-reliance using energy efficiency and renewable energy sources enable greater resilience in the face of repression. Technologies that enable reliable communication independently of governments, and which prevent government surveillance, help support nonviolent resistance to repression.

---

75 An example is limited US government financial support for the Serbian student movement Otpor that led a nonviolent campaign that ousted the country's leader Slobodan Milošević in 2000.

Many different social movements have affinities with social defence

Nearly every major social movement promoting justice and equality has affinities with social defence. The most obvious is the peace movement: the idea of social defence is an outgrowth of efforts to oppose war and imagine alternatives. Many of the activists who have sought to promote social defence have been involved in the peace movement.

As noted, workers have a crucial role to play in social defence, so there is an important link with workers' movements, especially efforts to democratise the workplace and empower workers. Of special relevance is the movement for workers' control, in which workers take over management roles and the boss-worker hierarchy is replaced by cooperative arrangements. An aggressor can control industry most easily by coercing or replacing high-level bosses. When there are no bosses, taking over is far more difficult, especially if the workers maintain solidarity in resistance.

Movements for greater equality – the feminist movement, the occupy movement, anti-racist movements, movements for people with disabilities – build the sort of tolerance and support for diversity that is valuable for resisting repression.

In these and other ways, today's social movements are helping to lay the basis for a social defence system.

Experience in nonviolent acion is an effective preparation for social defence

For many people, the very idea of social defence is strange, even absurd, because they assume that defence means military defence. Furthermore, they assume violence is always victorious against nonviolent opponents.

On the other hand, people who have participated in nonviolent actions – rallies, strikes or whatever – are usually much more receptive to the idea of social defence. Participating in protests can generate an appreciation of the power of collective action. This means that the idea of replacing the military by civilian resistance is not quite as strange as for those without personal experience.

The implication is that a highly effective way to promote social defence is to encourage more people to participate in nonviolent actions, accompanied by information about how nonviolence works.

Experience in nonviolent action is important, but on its own it is not the basis for social defence, which also involves specific training and preparation, including transforming organisations and technological systems. Even so, being involved in nonviolent action is so important that it should be part of efforts to transform systems.

Social defence can be accompanied by social attack

In the usual way of thinking, a social defence system does not have the capacity for offence. In this it is quite different from military systems: tanks, planes and missiles can be used for defence or offence. However, rallies and strikes cannot be used to attack distant opponents – at least not militarily, namely not with violence.

On the other hand, a social defence system provides the tools for a nonviolent attack against distant opponents. A strike or a boycott can be against an enterprise or product somewhere else. This is potentially potent when production chains extend across the globe. A strike by workers at a car component plant in one country can target a company or a government elsewhere.

More important than attack via noncooperation are two processes: persuasion and example. As a community develops its own capacity for nonviolent resistance to aggression, a high priority is building links with sympathetic groups elsewhere, especially in countries from which aggression might occur. Also important is fostering relationships with members of armed forces in potential aggressor countries.

With these sorts of links, any attempt by a foreign power to mount an invasion would be met by concerted efforts to mobilise resistance within the foreign country, for example by encouraging protests and disobedience to orders. If an invasion actually occurs, this same process can continue, with attempts to foster resistance and rebellion within the aggressor society and especially within its troops. The ultimate outcome of such an effort might even be a nonviolent overthrow of the rulers of the aggressor state.

Even without such an active effort to stir up resistance, the existence of a social defence system has an attack function purely by setting an example. People around the world can become aware of how communities can organise themselves to resist aggression and repression, and can think, "We can do that for ourselves."

The implication is that social defence should not be seen as purely defensive. If, as the saying goes, the best defence is a good offence, then social defence needs to include efforts to encourage challenges and alternatives to military systems elsewhere.[76] Promoting the idea of social defence is itself threatening to military-based systems.

Nonviolent action has four dimensions relevant to social defence

Stellan Vinthagen in his book *A Theory of Nonviolent Action* identifies four dimensions of nonviolent action, which he calls dialogue facilitation, power breaking, utopian enactment and normative regulation.[77] This way of understanding different aspects of nonviolent action can usefully be connected with social defence. The implication is that a social defence system should pay attention to all four dimensions.

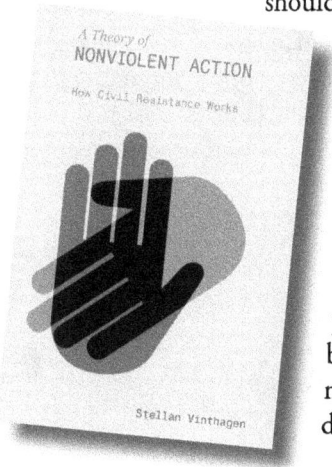

Dialogue facilitation refers to communication. This includes communication with opponents and with third parties. Social defence should put a priority on enabling skilful communication to deter aggression, defend against attacks and to build solidarity in support of community values.

Power breaking refers to actions that challenge power relationships. These actions include strikes, boycotts and other methods of resistance and noncooperation. Social defence is built around developing the capacity to use such methods.

Utopian enactment refers to the role of nonviolent action in realising visions of a desirable future. At a basic level, this means not using violence when pursuing a world without violence. For social defence, utopian enactment can go much further. It implies designing

76 Brian Martin, "Revolutionary social defence," *Bulletin of Peace Proposals*, vol. 22, no. 1, March 1991, pp. 97–105. See also Theodore Olson, "Social defence and deterrence: their interrelationship," *Bulletin of Peace Proposals*, vol. 16, no. 1, 1985, pp. 33–40, especially p. 38.

77 Stellan Vinthagen, *A Theory of Nonviolent Action: How Civil Resistance Works* (London: Zed Books, 2015).

political, economic and social systems to reflect values such as care for others, fairness and liberty. Of course, there can be disagreements about values and how society should be organised to reflect them. The point is that nonviolent action and social defence should be more than merely resisting aggression: they should be exemplifying the sort of world that resisters believe is worth defending. For example, utopian enactment might involve promoting economic equality prior to and within the resistance, so that those who are more advantaged make greater sacrifices.

Normative regulation means making nonviolent action the standard framework for understanding and valuing, so it becomes a dominant social norm. This would be a considerable shift from the present glorification of violence in various forums and rituals. Instead of having commemorations of war heroes and military victories, there would be greater attention to struggles waged without violence. Films would be less often showing the triumph of violence by good guys over violence by bad guys, and more often show the power of nonviolent action. Within many social movements, normative regulation is already occurring: violence is often stigmatised. However, in the wider culture there is a widespread belief that violence is necessary to defend against attack and that, when confronting those seen as enemies, those who use violence are to be admired. Changing attitudes towards violence – especially military violence – is part of what is necessary to promote and implement social defence.

5
Social defence in a changing world

Most of the writing about social defence was published in the 1950s through the 1980s, though there were some significant contributions before and after these times. The 1980s saw the greatest grassroots interest in social defence, accompanying the huge mobilisation against nuclear war in the same decade. Since the 1980s, quite a few things have changed. In this chapter we comment on some of the important changes that affect the possibility for and operation of social defence.

In commenting on changes, it is important to remember that in most respects the operation of a social defence system would be the same now as half a century ago. The basic idea is that people defend against aggression and repression without using violence, using methods of protest, persuasion, noncooperation and intervention.

The strategic situation

The Cold War was a confrontation between the forces of the Soviet bloc and those of the United States and its allies in Western Europe, "forces" here referring to troops and weapons but also economic and propaganda competition, including involvement in proxy wars such as in Vietnam. This competition was seen as between Communism (state socialism) and capitalist liberal democracy (representative government).

In Western Europe, where interest in social defence was the greatest – in Germany, Netherlands, France, Italy, Sweden, Austria and elsewhere – there was a widespread belief that an invasion from the east, led by the Soviet Union, was possible. Nearly everyone in government and the wider population believed that the only thing preventing such an invasion was Western military might. The idea of total disarmament was very much a minority position, with little or no credibility even in the peace movement.

The peace movement in the late 1970s and early 1980s was primarily a movement against nuclear weapons, not against arms more generally. Within the movement were many pacifists who opposed involvement in military systems, but the majority of participants focused on nuclear weapons.

The key point in relation to social defence is that there was a widespread belief in the danger of invasion and hence the need for some form of defence. If not military defence, then social defence could be a replacement.

In 1989, Communist regimes in Eastern Europe collapsed, a process in which nonviolent protests played a major role; there was little violence except in Romania.[78] Then in 1991, the Soviet Union disintegrated,[79] leading to the creation of over a dozen new countries, nearly all of which moved from state socialism to capitalism (though in Russia and elsewhere, this was a particularly nasty form of predatory capitalism). The transformations in the Soviet bloc meant that the threat of an invasion of Western Europe receded, if not entirely disappeared. The rationale for military defence against Soviet aggression dissipated, and hence also the motivation for a nonviolent alternative. Interest in social defence, which had never been all that great, declined dramatically.[80]

With the end of the Cold War, many observers expected there to be a "peace dividend," namely a reduction in military spending that would enable greater spending on education, health and consumer goods. However, Western military expenditures hardly declined at all. This could be a reflection of the strength of the military-industrial complex, a powerful coalition of corporate, military and government interest groups that maintained military spending. The primary pretext for military systems was gone, but the systems continued, searching for a new justification for their existence.

For a time, "humanitarian intervention" served as a rationale. Supposedly, military forces were needed to protect vulnerable populations, for example from civil wars. However, humanitarian intervention through nonviolent means never gained much support from governments. It only flourished through groups such as Peace Brigades International.

Terrorism eventually emerged as the most powerful new rationale for the military. Governments have turned the world's attention to the allegedly dire threat from terrorism (and a few rogue states or movements, like North Korea and Islamic State). Meanwhile, most of the killings in the world are

---

78 Michael Randle, *People Power: The Building of a New European Home* (Stroud, UK: Hawthorn, 1991).

79 See the account in chapter 3 of the 1991 Soviet coup.

80 Brian Martin, "Whatever happened to social defence?" *Social Alternatives,* vol. 33, no. 4, 2014, pp. 55–60.

due to governments themselves. Often their targets are their own people. Much of the killing by governments can be considered a type of terrorism, called "state terrorism."[81]

In essence, militaries now have only a fake justification, namely (non-state) terrorism. To deal with it, however, there is no need for tanks, destroyers, jets and missiles, or large numbers of troops. Many people think militaries are needed to defend against threats, so governments drum up fear about terrorism and hope few will notice that military spending has little to do with countering terrorism. Meanwhile, state terrorism is largely invisible, or just taken for granted.

Volunteer armies

Decades ago, in quite a few parts of the world, military service was mandatory. The process of forced recruitment is called conscription or, in the US, the draft. The prevalence of conscription varied quite a lot. In some countries, there was universal military service for young men, usually for a fixed period such as two years. In others, conscription was only introduced in wartime.

In countries with a high standard of living, conscription has become less and less common,[82] perhaps due to greater levels of education and independent thinking, so regimentation in military service is resented. For affluent young men, military service can be seen as a step down rather than a step up.

The decline in compulsory military service has contradictory implications for social defence. Serving in the army can be a process of indoctrination, of learning to accept orders, serve the state and treat others as enemies.

---

81 Noam Chomsky and Edward S. Herman, *The Political Economy of Human Rights* (Boston: South End Press, 1979); Frederick H. Gareau, *State Terrorism and the United States: From Counterinsurgency to the War on Terrorism* (Atlanta, GA: Clarity Press, 2004); Alexander George (ed.), *Western State Terrorism* (Cambridge: Polity Press, 1991); Michael Stohl and George A. Lopez (eds.), *The State as Terrorist: The Dynamics of Governmental Violence and Repression* (Westport, CT: Greenwood, 1984); Michael Stohl and George A. Lopez (eds.), *Terrible Beyond Endurance? The Foreign Policy of State Terrorism* (Westport, CT: Greenwood, 1988).

82 David Cortright and Max Watts, *Left Face: Soldier Unions and Resistance Movements in Modern Armies* (Westport, CT: Greenwood Press, 1991).

Peace movements have long campaigned against conscription, especially in wartime. This is partly a matter of fundamental principle: to oppose militarism and war, refusing military service is a matter of conscience. Opposing conscription is also an effective strategy. During the US military intervention in Vietnam, opposing conscription was a potent mode of refusal. Young men burned their draft cards as a symbolic and actual form of resistance.

In Norway, conscription existed for decades, but when young men claim conscientious objection to military service, they were required to serve in alternative service. In the 1970s, some pacifists went further and refused alternative service. These so-called "total resisters" launched a campaign to allow full refusal of any service to the state.[83]

Among those who applied and were accepted for alternative service, many demanded that the service should be focused on nonviolent alternatives to military defence. Norway, Sweden, Italy and Denmark were among those states where such demands were presented. In response, authorities in some of these countries made small symbolic gestures, for example by allowing a group to hear a single lecture about nonviolent alternatives or to publish articles about such alternatives in the group's government-funded journal. However, no authorities implemented serious training in nonviolent action.

Today, War Resisters' International continues to campaign against conscription and takes up the cause of objectors in countries around the world.

Despite the importance of opposing conscription, it should be recognised that it has some potential advantages from the point of view of social defence. When a considerable proportion of serving troops are conscripts, they are less prone to indoctrination and more susceptible to refusing orders, especially when they are commanded to undertake politically unpopular tasks. In chapter 3, we recounted the story of the Soviet invasion of Czechoslovakia

---

83 Majken Jul Sørensen, *Humour in Political Activism: Creative Nonviolent Resistance* (Palgrave Macmillan, 2016).

in 1968, during which many Soviet troops became "unreliable." These young conscripts were susceptible to appeals from Czechoslovaks who sought to convince them that the invasion was wrong.

In Italy during the 1980s, the peace movement was able to bring about a change in options for alternative service. Young men who refused military service – a universal obligation – could choose various forms of alternative service, including working towards social defence. Strangely, then, conscription provided strength to efforts for social defence, and the end of conscription led to a major decline in these efforts.[84]

A fully professional army, in which a large percentage of soldiers make the military their career, is probably less susceptible to fraternisation because most members are fully committed to their roles and are unlikely to risk their careers by resisting orders. However, it is uncertain how this might operate in practice. Some armies in earlier eras were sequestered in barracks and less exposed to popular opinion. Today's soldiers, older and more experienced, are more likely to live with their families and to be in touch with current events through mass and social media. Whether contemporary professional armies are reliable tools for repressing a population depends a lot on the circumstances.

There is also the question of the resistance of the military to moves towards social defence, which eventually would mean eliminating military defence. For some, this would be a threat to their careers and, even more, to their self-image. On the other hand, many of today's soldiers are highly skilled and could undertake other jobs. Furthermore, there would still be a role for some of the functions of today's troops, for example in emergency services. If any military specialists became committed to social defence, they would be the ideal advisers for developing systems to take into account the methods and thinking of possible aggressors.

New military technologies

Vast numbers of scientists, engineers, psychologists and others work at developing more effective weapons systems. The results include everything from specially designed bullets to missiles. Most of military research and development is oriented towards war-fighting, and thus not very relevant to using military forces against peaceful opponents.

---

84 Information provided by Antonino Drago.

Drones are a new development. The US military and intelligence services choose and track targets using camera surveillance and monitoring of communications. Then long-range killer drones are used to assassinate targets in places like Afghanistan, Iraq and Yemen, while decision-making and control are exercised by soldiers in the US, safe in their bunkers. This is an expanding feature of military operations against so-called terrorists in an undeclared war with no boundaries and no end in sight.

Drone killings are concerning for a number of reasons, including the lack of any attempt to deal with opponents through legal channels, killing of civilians and the counterproductive radicalisation of populations. It can be argued that drone killings are more individualised and therefore have fewer adverse impacts than indiscriminate bombings.[85] In any case, it seems unlikely that drone assassinations would be used intentionally against a community that had renounced the use of violence; if they were, this would greatly increase resistance.

Robotic warfare, in which armed weapons systems operate autonomously or semi-autonomously based on algorithms, raises a range of concerns. However, it seems unlikely that robot killers would be unleashed against civilian protesters and just as unlikely that robots would be developed to control civilian protest. Although unlikely, any social defence system would need to monitor developments in robotic warfare.

A significant component of research on military and police technologies has been devoted to what has been called the "technology of repression." This includes crowd-control technologies such as rubber bullets, water cannons, pepper spray, infrasound, concussion grenades, electroshock weapons and much else. Then there are technologies for imprisonment and torture, including leg irons, thumb screws, sensory deprivation and (again)

---

85 Rosa Brooks, *How Everything Became War and the Military Became Everything: Tales from the Pentagon* (New York: Simon & Schuster, 2016), provides insightful commentary about drone killings, robotic warfare and non-lethal weapons.

electroshock weapons. Also important are surveillance technologies, including anti-encryption programs, key loggers, facial identification software, vehicle tracking systems, voice identification programs and software for analysing networks.

These technologies sound nasty and many of them are. On the one hand, most of these technologies are designed to be "non-lethal," namely not to kill people but rather to control, hurt or monitor them. (They do sometimes cause death.) It is less lethal to be maimed by a rubber bullet than killed by a regular bullet or a bomb. The advantage of being non-lethal, from the point of view of forces using the weapons, is that they are seen as more acceptable. Some of the weapons leave no traces or are hard to document and therefore are harder to expose. Beating someone on the soles of their feet, called bastinado, leaves no obvious traces and thus is harder to expose as torture. (This is a technology in the sense of a technique.) Pepper spray can cause intense pain but no obvious injury: no blood or bruises.

The crowd control and torture technologies can be effective in repression, but they are not anything new from the point of view of nonviolent protest. When protesters are obviously nonviolent, then weapons used against them seem unfair to many observers, as shown by the now-famous incident in which a police officer was filmed pepper-spraying non-resisting students.[86] Torture, whatever weapons are used, is widely seen as wrong, at least when used against nonviolent opponents. The basis of the campaigns by Amnesty International is that imprisonment and torture of nonviolent campaigners is to be condemned as a human rights violation. When torture is documented and exposed, many people are outraged.[87]

When repression is severe and public protest runs the risk of heavy-handed police tactics, it is often better to shift to tactics of dispersal such

---

86 "UC Davis student protesters pepper sprayed," https://www.youtube.com/watch?v=6AdDLhPwpp4.

87 On the dynamics of outrage over torture, and torture technology, see Aloysia Brooks, *The Annihilation of Memory and Silent Suffering: Inhibiting Outrage at the Injustice of Torture in the War on Terror in Australia* (PhD thesis, University of Wollongong, 2017); Brian Martin and Steve Wright, "Countershock: mobilizing resistance to electroshock weapons," *Medicine, Conflict and Survival*, vol. 19, no. 3, July-September 2003, pp. 205–222; Brian Martin and Steve Wright, "Looming struggles over technology for border control," *Journal of Organisational Transformation and Social Change*, vol. 3, no. 1, 2006, pp. 95–107.

as strikes and boycotts, for which crowd control technologies are irrelevant.

The technologies of surveillance are a significant tool against any protest movement. However, in developing a social defence system, they are readily taken into account. Technological systems can be designed to counter surveillance by making communications secure, for example through encryption. Just as important is decentralising the capacity for decision-making and leadership. It has long been the case that governments may arrest leaders of movements, and surveillance technologies make it easier to identify low-profile leaders. However, if the movement does not depend on leaders, it is resilient against surveillance and arrest of key individuals, because many participants are skilled and ready to take leadership roles.

Because leadership and decision-making are potential targets, ensuring these in the face of repression is vital. However, this is a long-standing challenge, and technologies of surveillance do not change things very much.

The rise of nonviolent action

Nonviolent action has been used for centuries. However, it was only in the 1900s that nonviolent action was conceptualised as a form of struggle that could be the basis for campaigns against injustice. Gandhi was the crucial figure, developing nonviolent campaigns with a strategic goal.

Gradually, the conscious use of nonviolent action became more widely adopted. The US civil rights movement raised awareness dramatically, and also stimulated the expansion of nonviolence training, in which people preparing for action would learn and practise relevant skills.[88]

88 For example, *Handbook for Nonviolent Campaigns* (War Resisters' International, 2009).

Since the 1930s, there have been spontaneous nonviolent insurrections that have toppled dictatorships, but most of these episodes were not widely known, nor thought of in terms of nonviolent struggle.[89] Gradually more information about such struggles became available, and more campaigners became familiar with relevant methods and training.

The movement against nuclear power helped spread experience with nonviolence training, starting with action against the Seabrook nuclear power plant in New Hampshire in 1976.[90] The anti-nuclear-power movement was worldwide, and information about successful campaigns was shared widely, so there was a mutual process of learning and inspiration between campaigns in Europe, North America, Australia, Japan and elsewhere.

Gradually, more social movements became knowledgeable about and committed to nonviolent action, while the allure of armed struggle declined. The labour, feminist, peace and environmental movements, among others, have been primarily nonviolent in practice. Furthermore, there has been an increase in understanding of the dynamics of nonviolent struggle.

The end of the Cold War helped discredit state socialism and armed struggle, giving greater opportunities for nonviolent action as a means for social change. The global justice movement (more commonly called the anti-globalisation movement) received a major boost in the actions in Seattle in 1999, putting nonviolence ideas into a range of associated movements.

In the aftermath of the collapse of state socialism, there were movements in several post-socialist countries to overthrow dictators, in Serbia in 2000 and then Georgia, Ukraine and elsewhere, in the so-called coloured revolutions. There was considerable sharing of experiences, especially by veterans of the Serbian movement Otpor, that further spread ideas about nonviolent action.[91]

---

89 For example, Patricia Parkman, *Insurrectionary Civic Strikes in Latin America 1931–1961* (Cambridge, MA: Albert Einstein Institution, 1990).

90 Barbara Epstein, *Political Protest and Cultural Revolution: Nonviolent Direct Action in the 1970s and 1980s* (Berkeley: University of California Press, 1991).

91 Srdja Popovic, Andrej Milivojevic and Slobodan Djinovic, *Nonviolent Struggle: 50 Crucial Points* (Belgrade: Centre for Applied NonViolent Action and Strategies, 2007); Srdja Popovic, Slobodan Djinovic, Andrej Milivojevic, Hardy Merriman, and Ivan Marovic, *CANVAS Core Curriculum: A Guide to Effective Nonviolent Struggle* (Belgrade: Centre for Applied Nonviolent Action and Strategies, 2007).

The work of Gene Sharp has been important. Many of his writings inspired campaigners in different parts of the world; his book *From Dictatorship to Democracy* was translated into numerous languages. The ideas of Gandhi also continued to be influential.

In 2011, the nonviolent uprisings in Tunisia, Egypt and other countries in North Africa and west Asia – called the Arab spring – captured the attention of the Western media and for the first time put nonviolent action into mainstream discourse.

For decades, scholarly interest in nonviolent action was a marginal pursuit, with only a few dozen individuals across the globe undertaking research. In the 2000s, interest increased greatly, partly due to the increased use of nonviolent action in campaigning and partly due to the impact of the work of Erica Chenoweth and Maria Stephan, which challenged the usual assumption that violence is more effective than nonviolent action.[92]

It is reasonable to say that nonviolent action, in practice and in research activity, has moved from being mostly unrecognised to being standard practice within many social movements. This has occurred with little support from governments, corporations or other major groups, and despite lack of media coverage and lack of understanding by many people unconnected with activism. The use of nonviolent action has blossomed despite being largely a voluntary enterprise. Not having wealthy or powerful backers may be an advantage, preventing co-option by groups with other agendas.

Social defence is basically the use of nonviolent action to defend communities against aggression and repression, with an associated elimination of military systems. The massive expansion in the awareness of and use of nonviolent action means that there is a greater capacity for social defence. However, this has not yet translated into any serious moves to replace military systems with nonviolent alternatives.

As social movements have become more committed to nonviolent action, some left-wing critics have alleged that nonviolent action actually protects governments.[93] In particular, the critics allege that the US government is behind some of the popular movements to overthrow repressive regimes. In our view, these critics lack an understanding of the revolutionary potential

---

92 Erica Chenoweth and Maria J. Stephan, *Why Civil Resistance Works: The Strategic Logic of Nonviolent Conflict* (New York: Columbia University Press, 2011).

93 The best known critic is Peter Gelderloos, *How Nonviolence Protects the State* (Cambridge, MA: South End Press, 2007).

of nonviolent action, and do not recognise the degree to which the use of violence, especially in armed struggle, can undermine egalitarian goals.[94] Even so, it is useful to remember that there is no guarantee that nonviolent action will be used only for good causes, and to be aware that the more nonviolent action is used, the more likely criticisms will be voiced.

Increased sophistication of opponents of nonviolent movements

As social movements have become more aware of nonviolent action and more capable in using it, some governments have become more sophisticated in dealing with nonviolent movements.[95] This is especially true of more repressive governments, which might otherwise be vulnerable to nonviolent challenges.

When police or military use violence against unarmed protesters, this has the potential of rebounding against the attackers in what Gene Sharp calls political jiu-jitsu. When governments become aware of this dynamic, they can be more careful about their use of violence.

The widespread use of digital media means that government censorship is less effective. Activists can use their phones to make videos of beatings, killings and atrocities. One way that governments can counter negative information is by spreading disinformation through social media, for example claims that photos have been staged or that well known activists are terrorist sympathisers. Rather than censorship, governments can produce a flood of confusing or irrelevant information, leading citizens to give up trying to make sense of it.

---

94 For a critical review of Gelderloos's book, see Brian Martin, "How nonviolence is misrepresented," *Gandhi Marg*, vol. 30, no. 2, July-September 2008, pp. 235–257. See also Jørgen Johansen, Brian Martin and Matt Meyer, "Non-violence versus US imperialism," *Economic & Political Weekly*, vol. 47, no. 38, 22 September 2012, pp. 82–89.

95 Excellent treatments include Erica Chenoweth, "Trends in nonviolent resistance and state response: is violence towards civilian-based movements on the rise?" *Global Responsibility to Protect*, vol. 9, 2017, pp. 86–100; William J. Dobson, *The Dictator's Learning Curve: Inside the Global Battle for Democracy* (New York: Doubleday, 2012); Zeynep Tufekci, *Twitter and Tear Gas: The Power and Fragility of Networked Protest* (New Haven, CT: Yale University Press, 2017), chapter 9, "Governments strike back."

Repressive governments have become better at giving the appearance of being fair. Rather than hold elections that are obviously staged because regime candidates receive 99% of the vote, elections are swayed in less obvious ways, for example by using bureaucratic procedures to make it difficult for opponents to rent office space, obtain media coverage or put names on ballots. When regime candidates win with 55% of the vote, this seems more plausibly to be fair and causes less scepticism.

Governments can intervene in organising before movements gain momentum, for example by setting up fake groups that support the government, by infiltrating groups and causing dissension, and by gathering discrediting private information about key activists and using it to blackmail them. They can encourage movements to use violence, for example by using attack methods that are provocative.

Nearly all these techniques have been used for a long time. What is different is that some governments have a better understanding of nonviolent movements and are becoming more experienced in countering them. This should not be surprising. The interaction between governments and social movements can be considered to be a strategic encounter, with each side doing what it can to be successful in its own terms. As governments become more sophisticated in their repressive techniques, some of which do not even seem repressive, movements need to be innovative.

Any group wanting to promote social defence needs to be aware that opponents can try new techniques, learn from experience and become more effective. When social defence is just an idea, its proponents may be left alone. When citizen capacities become greater, there may be more resistance. The key is to take into account what others might do.

The Internet

In the 1990s, the Internet became widely used. For current generations, it can seem difficult to imagine life without email, the web, Facebook, smartphones and all sorts of online applications. Nearly all the writing about social defence preceded the rise of the Internet, during a time when media meant the mass media and activists typically communicated using face-to-face meetings, letters (sent through the post, also known as snail mail), telephone and fax. An even earlier generation, prior to the 1980s, operated without desktop computers.

Means of communication can make a big difference to the capacity for resistance to repression. A key factor is whether communication systems are broadcast or network, in other words one-directional or multi-directional. Radio and television are broadcast media: a small number of producers and editors control content that goes to a large audience. In contrast, the telephone and email are network media: individuals can send messages to each other without anyone controlling the content. This is a crucial difference.

Broadcast media are especially suited for rulers: they can control what information is available to the population. For this reason, it is common that in military coups, the first targets for takeover are radio and television stations.[96]

Network media are suited for resistance to repression. People can communicate with each other to share information and organise actions. Rulers have limited options. If they shut down an entire communications system, this is highly disruptive and can trigger greater opposition.

During the 2011 uprising against Egyptian dictator Hosni Mubarak, he shut down the Internet. Resisters used various means to work around the shutdown. Meanwhile, because online information sources were cut off, many people not involved in the uprising went to the streets to find out what was happening, thus increasing the scale of the protests. This example shows that a communications medium that is widely used for private or commercial purposes can be helpful for resisters, whereas a specially designed resistance communication system would be more vulnerable to disruption.

It is now easy to take photographs and videos and immediately share them. This gives unprecedented capacity for documenting and exposing human rights abuses.

The Internet seems to be fostering different patterns of interaction. Face-to-face meetings are less necessary. Before mobile phones, people would make arrangements in advance, for example to meet at a particular time and

---

96 T. E. Finer, *The Man on Horseback: The Role of the Military in Politics* (London: Pall Mall Press, 1962); D. J. Goodspeed, *The Conspirators: A Study of the Coup d'État* (London: Macmillan, 1962).

place, whereas now it is more common to coordinate personal connections on the go. A group can organise a meeting – its location and time – while people are on their way to it. This enables "smart mobs," self-organising groups, that can be used for entertainment or political action.

Much more political activity happens online. Petitions used to be printed sheets circulated at meetings, public stalls or taken door to door. Now petitions are circulated online and large numbers of signatures can be obtained in a short time. This has both advantages and disadvantages.[97] The advantage is the ease by which large numbers of people can become aware of issues and express their views. The disadvantage is a lower level of engagement. Signing is so easy that commitment may be superficial. This was also true of petitions in the past, but at least in door-to-door canvassing there often was a conversation and a brief personal connection.

Not everything about the Internet and social media is positive for social defence purposes. They have provided governments and corporations with new capacities for monitoring individuals. Surveillance can occur through emails and texts, social media postings, financial transactions and security cameras. Spy agencies have the ability to collect massive amounts of data and to use it to identify patterns of interaction. If an individual comes under suspicion, their communications with others can be monitored. Intensive surveillance can be difficult to avoid. For example, a keystroke logger can be remotely installed on a computer or phone so that messages can be monitored, and passwords intercepted. Social defence planning, in designing and training for the use of communication systems, needs to address both the positives and negatives of digital media.

Neoliberalism

Since the 1980s, a variant of capitalism called neoliberalism has been highly influential. In practice, governments have reduced their commitment to services, typically by selling government bodies or putting services out to tender. Corporations are more influential in shaping government policy, while trade unions and citizen groups are weakened. Barriers to international

---

97   Hahrie Han, *How Organizations Develop Activists: Civic Associations and Leadership in the 21st Century* (Oxford: Oxford University Press, 2014); Zeynep Tufekci, *Twitter and Tear Gas: The Power and Fragility of Networked Protest* (New Haven, CT: Yale University Press, 2017).

trade have been reduced, enabling transnational corporations to move production to locations with cheaper labour.

Although governments have divested themselves of some functions, they have also become more controlling in core functions including military operations, policing, border control and surveillance of citizens. Neoliberalism poses as reducing the role of government but actually helps governments serve the interests of the rich and powerful. A characteristic outcome of neoliberalism is greater economic inequality within countries.

How neoliberalism affects the potential for social defence is complex, involving several aspects. To begin, neoliberalism has accentuated a trend towards individualism and self-centreness and a decline in commitment to collective provision and mutual support. This definitely weakens the capacity of communities to resist aggression and repression. People are less likely to see their future as one of service to the common good, though there are still many such public-minded people. This is a trend, not a fait accompli.

Corporate globalisation has brought about a global division of labour. For quite a few products, like cars, different components are manufactured in different countries or locations and put together and sold in others. This reduces the self-reliance of any given population. Interconnected operations might seem beneficial for resistance, except that the interconnections are managed by corporate elites, not by workers and communities. When vital functions are dependent on global production chains, local communities are vulnerable.

On the other hand, militaries are also more dependent on global production chains. It is possible to imagine workers in one country interrupting production and transport of military equipment in another.

One of the targets of privatisation is military forces and police. In the traditional conception of the state, the army and the police are central to maintaining the state's monopoly on legitimate violence. Nevertheless, some governments are contracting out these core functions. For example, the US government hired thousands of military "contractors" – who in earlier times would have been called mercenaries – for its occupation of Iraq. Eventually these outnumbered the government-employed troops. In policing, it is now common for private security guards to carry out functions.

There are various debates about the significance of this partial privatisation of military and police forces. One argument by critics is that the private operatives are no longer accountable to the government: they can more easily avoid penalties for crimes. Whatever the judgement about such matters, our interest here is in the implications for social defence. Are military contractors and private security guards reliable when directed to take action against an unarmed population? What fraternisation techniques would be effective? If offered higher pay and better conditions for "defecting" (resigning from their contracts) and joining the resistance, would they be receptive? There is very little evidence about such questions.

Surveys of contractors suggest they are less concerned about money than doing their job professionally.[98] Many are former military personnel. Although some contractors have been involved in atrocities, this has been in a war context. An initial guess is that contractors, when confronted by nonviolent resistance, will respond similarly to government troops.

Conclusion

There have been many changes since the 1950s–1980s, the period of greatest activity in the articulation and promotion of social defence. The strategic situation is now dramatically different, there are new technologies enabling surveillance, and conscription has been abolished in many countries. Although some of these developments have made nonviolent resistance more difficult, overall the changes make social defence even more feasible than it was decades ago.

Probably the most important change is the much greater awareness and use of nonviolent action. Large numbers of activists, in all sorts of movements, have become familiar with the dynamics of nonviolent protest. Associated with this, armed struggle for taking state power is largely discredited in many countries. It is useful to remember that the very idea of strategic nonviolence for social change is quite new, being a product of Gandhi's campaigns in South Africa and India. Military strategy, in contrast, has a long history.

---

98 Volker Franke and Marc von Boemcken, "Guns for hire: motivations and attitudes of private security contractors," *Armed Forces & Society,* vol. 37, no. 4, 2011, pp. 725–742.

Nonviolent struggle, being relatively new and still unfamiliar to much of the population, remains in a developmental stage, with new understandings and applications occurring regularly. This is the greatest hope for the future.

The most important technological change relevant to social defence is the emergence of the Internet and associated network communication technologies. This has made it far easier for people to acquire information about nonviolence and to coordinate nonviolent campaigns.

Considering these changes that make social defence more promising than before, why has it fallen off the agenda? The answer lies in the factors that have remained unchanged. Most fundamental is the belief in the superiority of violence and the necessity for military defence. This belief has enabled the continuation of massive military spending despite the collapse of state socialism and the dramatic decline in the danger of foreign military invasion, at least so far as rich countries are concerned.

This points to a deeper factor. Militaries and police forces are fundamental to the current world order in which there is enormous economic and social inequality. Social defence involves empowering the people to be able to resist aggression and repression, and the skills and knowledge to do this can readily be turned against oppressive employers and unfair government policies. Therefore it is in the interests of current power-holders for people to believe in the need for military preparedness rather than the expansion of grassroots democracy. This helps explain why the threat of terrorism has been so greatly exaggerated, why nonviolent approaches to addressing terrorism have been ignored by governments, and why governments have given so little support to nonviolent alternatives. Social defence remains a radical alternative.

6
Movements

There are many important social movements, among them anti-regime, environmental, peace, labour, human rights and feminist movements. How can social movements help build a capacity for social defence? And what can thinking in terms of social defence do to help movements become more effective?

A movement, as the name suggests, involves a considerable number of people acting towards a shared goal. For the feminist movement, for example, this means acting towards greater equality between women and men. Movements are seldom unified. Some feminists primarily seek equality of opportunity within current social structures whereas others seek changes in these structures so that they are shaped by values such as cooperation and compassion. Then there can be debates about what constitute "women's values," and so on.

Movements have been highly influential. The abolitionist movement was central in the ending of slavery, which for centuries had been accepted as natural. The environmental movement has created a consciousness about the value of nature and the need to protect and preserve it. There are also more focused movements within the environmental movement, for example the movement against nuclear power.

So how does social defence fit in? Currently, there is very little organised action towards social defence, so it exists primarily as a latent potential and as an idea that can inform campaigns. There is no social movement to promote social defence.

In this chapter, we discuss several social movements that have potential connections with social defence. This is a selective treatment, because for each social movement there is a vast amount of activity and commentary. However, very little of this is explicitly about social defence. Accordingly, our comments here are preliminary and exploratory.

The feminist movement

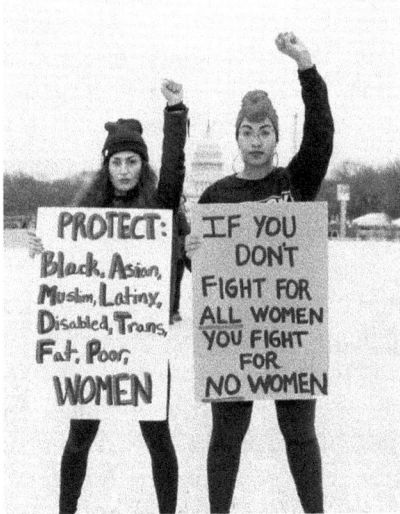

Feminism has challenged the subordination of women and asserted the importance of some traditionally feminine characteristics such as compassion and caring. How this relates to social defence is complex.

The first point to note is that men are far more likely to use violence than women. Most soldiers are men, most murders are by men and most family violence is by men. It should also be noted that men are often the victims as well as the perpetrators. On the front lines in wars, men kill other men, and much interpersonal violence is between men.

There is a long history of women playing prominent roles in nonviolent struggles, and indeed in promoting the use of nonviolent methods.[99] Anne-Marie Codur and Mary Elizabeth King, in recounting a great number of historical examples, offer five reasons why women have an advantage over men in nonviolent movements.

1. When women are present, security forces are less likely to use violence.
2. Women are often better able to maintain nonviolent discipline.

---

99 A classic reference is Pam McAllister, *The River of Courage: Generations of Women's Resistance and Action* (Philadelphia: New Society Press, 1991).

3. Women, more than men, prefer non-hierarchical networks, which are better suited to nonviolent movements.

4. Women are less prone to rivalry within movements and can build greater unity.

5. Women are better able to foster solidarity across class, ethnic, religious and other divisions.[100]

Feminism, in many of its strands, rejects interpersonal violence and asserts the importance of building relationships, of compassion and caring for others. In the peace movement and many other social justice movements, women have played significant roles.

That women are more involved in caring roles may have a biological basis in their capacity to have children. Whatever the judgement about innate tendencies, many of the differences between women and men are learned as part of culture and socialisation. There is no doubt that women have the capacity to be violent and cruel. Therefore, when praising and advocating the uptake of feminine values of caring and compassion, it is worth noting that many men have developed these values and some women have not. The point of a feminist agenda is to shape social structures and interactions around such values that, historically, have been associated with women.[101]

One thing the feminist movement can contribute to social defence is a continual emphasis on values including caring, empathy and human connection. In discussing and promoting social defence, there is a risk of focusing exclusively on practical, instrumental techniques, everything from social ostracism to shutting down factories, and forgetting about the human factor. This is perhaps especially a concern when social defence is seen as a direct replacement for military defence, given that military systems are based on a systematic rejection of caring and compassion for the enemy. Exactly what it means to have a caring and compassionate defence system remains to be learned.

There is another strand of feminism that sees equality primarily as

---

100 Anne-Marie Codur and Mary Elizabeth King, "Women in civil resistance," in Miriam M. Kurtz and Lester R. Kurtz (eds.), *Women, War, and Violence: Topography, Resistance, and Hope, Volume 2* (Praeger, 2015), pp. 401–446, at p. 433.

101 For various perspectives on feminism and nonviolence, see Pam McAllister (ed.), *Reweaving the Web of Life: Feminism and Nonviolence* (Philadelphia: New Society Publishers, 1982).

women having equal opportunity to fill standard social roles. This includes roles as soldiers and rulers. In the past several decades, there has been a push in some countries for women to be allowed in the military and to have equal access to all positions, including front-line combat. In Israel, for example, all women as well as men are required to serve in the military.

There are some obvious limits to the desirability of women having equal access to roles, because some roles should be abolished. Becoming a torturer is an example. What feminist would argue that women should be given the same opportunities as men to become torturers? Then there are serial killers and paedophiles.

From a pacifist point of view, using violence against others is wrong. Pacifists historically have refused military service, and some have gone to prison because of their refusal. From a social defence perspective, the goal should be for armies to be replaced by popular nonviolent resistance, which means that neither women nor men would be soldiers.

At this point, it is worth noting that when organised violence is abolished, there will still be roles requiring high-level training, physical strength and courage, especially emergency response to disasters such as fires, earthquakes and floods. There will still be roles for search and rescue. Currently, these tasks are mostly carried out by men. A feminist agenda would be to make them equally accessible and attractive to women.

When feminism meets social defence, the implication is that equality in current roles is not always a desirable goal, because some current roles are undesirable for anyone. Feminism needs to be tempered or shaped by other agendas, and one of them is nonviolence.

The environmental movement

Like other movements, environmentalism has many facets. It can be manifest in campaigns to preserve areas of nature, to protect species, to restrain global warming, to oppose nuclear power, and a host of other issues. The common theme is that instead of humans dominating nature, they should live in harmony with it, treating all aspects of nature as having value, though not necessarily equal value.

Environmentalists have a strong reason to be anti-militarists: world military operations impose one of the major impacts on the environment through energy use, destruction of habitat, and pollution. Many people have heard about the 1989 Exxon Valdez oil spill in the Arctic. Not so many have heard that ten times as much oil was released during the first Gulf war in 1991. Then there are nuclear weapons, with the potential to destroy and contaminate vast areas of the earth and kill untold numbers of animals as well as humans.

To this, social defence adds another dimension. For resistance against aggression and repression, it is advantageous for communities to be self-reliant in food, water, energy and transport. This is because an occupying force, to subordinate the population, can exert power by controlling these vital areas. Self-reliance means being able to cope largely through local resources and networks; it is not the same as self-sufficiency, which means total independence, and is almost impossible to achieve.

When an aggressor can control or destroy a few key facilities on which people depend, it is harder to resist. Key facilities include ports, airports, refineries, large power plants and large dams. Therefore, a community will be more resilient when food, water, energy and transport are not dependent on a few central facilities but instead are provided locally. This includes local food production, rainwater tanks, small-scale renewable energy systems, and housing planned around walking and cycling.

Many environmental campaigns have implications for fostering local self-reliance. For example, campaigns against pesticides contribute to a challenge to industrial agriculture, which involves massive monocultures, heavy machinery, pesticides, artificial fertilisers, genetically modified crops and long-distance transport to markets. Industrial agriculture is vulnerable to disruption by destroying or controlling access to any one of several inputs.

This can be contrasted to organic farming, which involves a variety of crops grown without pesticides or genetic modification. Organic farming is less vulnerable to disruption and therefore is better suited to a social defence system. Thus there is a commonality in environmental campaigning and promotion of social defence.

However, environmental goals do not automatically align with social defence. Consider renewable energy technologies. One option is large solar arrays at a considerable distance from end-users. Such arrays, though seldom as large as coal-fired or nuclear power plants, are more susceptible to disruption than rooftop solar panels. One solar energy proposal involves large satellites orbiting the earth and focusing a high-intensity beam to a receiver on the earth's surface. This is a form of renewable energy that would be an obvious target for terrorists or aggressors: by redirecting the beam, it could be used as a weapon. The lesson here is that the key to supporting the capacity for social defence is not whether an energy system is sustainable but whether it is decentralised and easy for local users to build, install and maintain.

Another important connection between the environmental movement and social defence involves campaigning methods. Peak environmental organisations commonly operate within the political system, for example by lobbying, undertaking research, providing information and encouraging members to adopt sustainable lifestyles. Supplementing this mainstream approach, the environmental movement includes many groups that use methods of nonviolent direct action such as rallies, boycotts, occupations and blockades. Forest activists have undertaken daring actions, for example sitting in precarious tripods high above the ground or locking themselves to equipment. These and many other actions have aided environmental causes and fostered skills in and understandings of nonviolent action.

The environmental movement therefore has two important links to social defence. First, the elements of the movement that promote local self-reliance in energy, food, water and transport improve the capacity of communities to resist aggression and repression. Second, some environmental campaigning involves use of nonviolent action, providing understanding and skills that can be used for defence against aggression.

In some cases, it might be said that environmental campaigning *is* social defence, in the sense that it opposes repressive action by the state. Nuclear power is a technology that, because of the possibility of catastrophic accidents and terrorist or criminal uses of nuclear materials, requires security against threats. A society heavily dependent on nuclear power is likely to include extensive surveillance and policing operations to protect against possible threats, and their surveillance and policing capacity can be turned against anti-nuclear protesters and others.[102] Massive police clampdowns

---

102 Michael Flood and Robin Grove-White, *Nuclear Prospects: A Comment on the Individual, the State and Nuclear Power* (London: Friends of the Earth, 1976).

have been used against some anti-nuclear protests, for example Wyhl in Germany in the early 1970s. Aside from its environmental impacts, nuclear power brings with it greater government repression, and that is exactly what social defence is designed to defend against.

Environmental campaigners thus have some experience in resisting repression. They can learn from the idea of social defence about how to become more systematic and wide-ranging in making their campaigns serve the dual goals of environmental protection and defence of communities against aggression and repression.

The labour movement

Workers have an incredible amount of power. Their efforts keep society operating, everything from food production to childcare. Without their skills, electricity systems would fail, financial transactions would be obstructed and goods would not be delivered to markets. By withdrawing their labour, workers can interfere with routine activities.

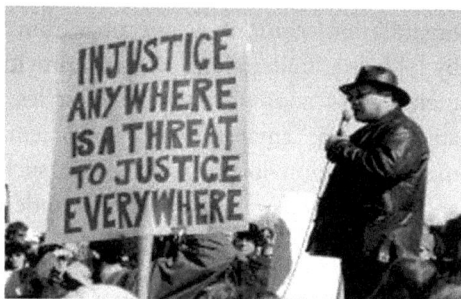

Some work is more critical than others. If teachers go on strike, students miss their classes but they can continue studying if they like. If hairdressers go on strike, people's hair won't look as nice but their lives can continue. But some occupations are vital, including workers in airports, ports, power plants and factories. If such workers go on strike, they can hold society to ransom. By the same token, workers are crucial players in resistance to aggression and repression. In a social defence system, workers are central figures.

In setting up a social defence system, ideally a community can survive even if an aggressor seizes control of crucial installations. Rather than depend on a few large power plants, energy can be supplied by local renewable sources, and energy efficiency measures ensure that demand is low. But for the time being, there are bound to be some important facilities that might be targeted in a takeover. Workers need to be prepared to stop production as a form of resistance.

Aggressors seldom have the capacity to run vital facilities themselves. Suppose there is a factory producing bicycles. (Why would an aggressor want to control a bicycle factory? That's another question.) It involves obtaining raw materials and parts from a variety of suppliers, putting together bicycles and distributing them to retailers. The factory requires water and electricity among other basic resources. It requires various communication technologies to ensure efficient operations.

The aggressors might say to the manager, "Do what we want or we will torture you and your children," so the manager cooperates. Or perhaps the aggressors simply fire the manager and install one of their own people. These are the two main methods used for control: intimidation to compel cooperation or replacement of key personnel.

Suppose the aim of the aggressor is to use everything produced by the factory for its own purposes. In the Nazi occupation of Europe, factories were used to produce weapons, vehicles and other products to serve the Nazi regime. Resistance was risky. Some workers sabotaged production, but in a subtle way so it seemed like an unavoidable breakdown. Alternatively, they worked more slowly than they might have, thus reducing output.

In a social defence system, preparations could be made so that resistance could be far more effective. One possibility is for the factory to rely on some crucial component that, if disabled, could not be easily restored, with a replacement held in a remote location, perhaps another country. The crucial component might be some code held in the cloud with the location and password held by supporters far from the factory. In such a situation, production can be stopped by disabling the component. Torture would be pointless because it would not get things going again.

Another possibility is not having bosses. There is a radical tradition in labour activism that advocates that workers collectively make all decisions about work, including how the work is carried out and what is produced. This is called workers' control or workers' self-management. It goes beyond what is commonly called industrial democracy, in which workers have representatives on councils that nominally oversee a workplace. In workers' control, bosses in the usual sense are replaced by systems in which workers cooperatively make decisions about running things.[103]

---

103 Gerry Hunnius, G. David Garson and John Case (eds.), *Workers' Control: A Reader on Labor and Social Change* (New York: Vintage, 1973); Ernie Roberts, *Workers' Control* (London: Allen & Unwin, 1973); H. B. Wilson, *Democracy and the*

There are quite a few historical examples of workers' control, especially in revolutionary situations, for example in Spain in the late 1930s. There are also instances in which workers in a particular workplace take control, for example in Britain in the 1960s. There are a few cases in which owners have gradually ceded decision-making power to workers. In the famous case of Lucas Aerospace in Britain in the 1980s, workers developed plans for products, including ones that would benefit the community.[104] Today, Mondragon in Spain is commonly cited as an example of worker participation, though in practice it combines features of self-management with features of traditional managerial hierarchy.

There is some research showing that productivity increases when workers have more control.[105] Despite this, employers have shown intense antagonism to workers' control, which is not surprising: it means that bosses lose their power and privileges. Local outbreaks of workers' control are typically met with state repression, sometimes with troops brought in to put managers back in control.

The idea of workers' control can be broadened to become worker-community control. What workers do is not just for themselves: what they produce is typically sold or provided to consumers. As shown in the case of Lucas Aerospace, workers are likely to be attuned to community interests rather than just serving the interests of the workers themselves.

Worker-community control is ideal for social defence, because it devolves power and makes it harder for any small group to take control. Without a single boss with the power to hire and fire – such decisions would be made collectively – an aggressor cannot take control simply by threatening or replacing the top boss.

In a social defence system, many people need to have skills, so that if leaders are arrested, killed or coerced by threats, others can step forward to take their place. Evidence from experience with workers' control suggests that workers, when they have a major say, are likely to give each other opportunities to learn and undertake different roles. This makes jobs more

Work Place (Montreal: Black Rose Books, 1974).

104 Hilary Wainwright and Dave Elliott, *The Lucas Plan: A New Trade Unionism in the Making?* (London: Allison and Busby, 1982).

105 Seymour Melman, *Decision-making and Productivity* (Oxford: Basil Blackwell, 1958).

interesting, fosters mutual support among workers – and gives greater capacity for nonviolent resistance.

What this means in practice can vary considerably depending on the type of workplace. In a factory, it might be redesigning the production process so that the skills of workers are increased and the work is made more interesting. In an office, it might mean designing the work tasks and operational systems so that decisions are made closer to the clients. In a hospital, it might mean greater equality between doctors, nurses, clerical and cleaning staff. In each workplace, preparing for social defence has significant ramifications.

Looking at the role of workers in social defence makes its radical implications obvious. For social defence, hierarchical organisational structures are a weakness, because leaders can be removed or coerced. So to take full advantage of the benefits of flatter organisations, in which workers have a great deal of independence and can collectively take initiatives, moving to a social defence system means transforming the usual top-down systems.

There is a connection here with military systems. Conventional military forces are based on a system of command. Individual soldiers and low-level units might have some degree of autonomy but only within the overall hierarchy. The same applies to many companies and government departments. Enlightened management gives low-level workers some scope for creativity and initiative but only within the parameters set by upper management. There is thus an organisational similarity between conventional military systems and conventional workplaces. Besides, the military is a workplace of its own.

In many countries, workplace hierarchies are protected against major challenges by legal arrangements, themselves backed ultimately by the military and police. If workers get together to take control, the government will take whatever measures are required to bring this rebellion under control. This is why a general strike – a strike by all workers, shutting down all services – is seen as revolutionary. It is also why strikes are often used in nonviolent challenges to repressive governments.

Social defence, to be fully effective, involves trusting workers to defend the interests of society as a whole. Because introducing social defence involves phasing out military defence, it also means removing the use of the military to defend the government against challengers. After all, a strike can be deployed against an aggressor or against the government.

Given that military and civilian workplace hierarchies are deeply entrenched, it seems that social defence is utopian. Indeed, it is unrealistic to imagine it will be brought in by a crusading government. Instead, it is more useful to see social defence as a goal or guidepost for campaigns today. For the labour movement, this means campaigning not just for better pay and conditions but also for workers to have more control over how the work is carried out and over its purpose.

The business movement

When supporters of social justice think about social movements, they commonly think of anti-racist, feminist, environmental and other such movements: ones that liberate groups subject to domination. However, there is nothing inherent in social movements to make them "progressive," and in any case the concepts of progress and liberation make implicit judgements about what is worthwhile.

There are many other sorts of movements, in opposite directions, for example fascist movements, the anti-feminist men's movement and armed Islamic movements. There are also some other types. In the early days of computing, it was possible to talk of a computerisation movement, to promote the use of computers wherever possible.[106] It's also possible to talk of a militarisation movement, promoting military values and solutions to social problems.

Many social justice campaigns tend to see their opponents as being part of an establishment, often as conservatives that are obstructing change. This perspective misses important processes: the so-called establishment is far from rigid, and often involves active efforts to promote different values. Neoliberalism, a political philosophy putting markets and corporate

---

106   Rob Kling and Suzanne Iacono, "The mobilization of support for computerization: the role of computerization movements," *Social Problems,* vol. 35, 1988, pp. 226–243.

hierarchies as central values, can readily fit some definitions of social movements. It is a movement that (according to critics) promotes the interests of elites rather than the interests of workers and citizens. Neoliberalism is not conservative in the sense of preserving traditional values. It is highly radical because it breaks down family and community structures, replacing them with commercial transactions.

Our aim in looking at social movements is to see how they might contribute to social defence. Obviously some movements are contrary or hostile to social defence, such as fascist and militarisation movements. But what about business?

Gene Sharp in his classic book *The Politics of Nonviolent Action* lists a large number of methods of nonviolent action, including dozens of types of strikes and boycotts. It is seldom appreciated how many of these involve businesses and other associations. Examples include a producers' boycott, refusal to let or sell property, a traders' boycott, and refusal to pay debts.

Consider, for example, what is sometimes called a "capital strike," which is when companies refuse to make investments. Capital strikes are commonly used to coerce governments into giving subsidies to business. They are a form of blackmail: "Either give us a better deal or we'll go elsewhere." However, capital strikes can be used for positive purposes. If a regime is repressive, businesses may stop making investments and instead move their capital and operations to other countries.

In today's world, large transnational companies are larger, in financial terms, than small countries, and hence potentially can have a large impact on governments and militaries. Most governments are highly sensitive to corporate interests because if a country's economy goes into decline, this may trigger popular unrest.

In practice, few large corporations become directly involved in challenging repressive governments. The classic case was foreign firms operating in Nazi Germany, some of which continued their businesses that served the Hitler's genocide. However, in recent decades there is greater attention to what is called "corporate social responsibility." This gives greater prospects that business leaders might take a stand against aggression and repression.

The international struggle against apartheid in South Africa shows the potential power of corporate activism. There was opposition to apartheid within South Africa, including armed resistance by the African National

Congress and nonviolent resistance by a range of groups. After decades of resistance, greater opposition developed outside of South Africa, taking many forms. One potent symbolic challenge was protests against South Africa's all-white sporting teams – cricket and rugby – in countries where they went to play international matches. Many governments imposed diplomatic sanctions. Then there was the international campaign to boycott trade and investment in South Africa. This actually hurt the oppressed black population, but was undertaken with the support of the South African organisations leading the resistance.[107]

Maintaining economic sanctions against the South African system was not easy. Most business leaders are primarily self-interested, so when the United Nations supported a boycott of oil imports to South Africa, some businesses tried to smuggle oil into the country, because there was money to be made. To maintain the boycott, these rogue businesses needed to be identified and shamed. This essentially involved activists and other businesses applying penalties in order to maintain adherence to the blockade.[108]

It is often thought that there is a natural affinity between businesses and the military or, more generally, between capitalism and militarism. However, the connection is less strong that it might seem. Arms manufacturers, naturally enough, have much to gain from military expenditures, and similarly for some other specialist industries, such as shipbuilding and surveillance technology. For many sectors of the economy, though, the military is primarily a drain. Farmers can sell food to soldiers, to be sure, but farmers would sell just as much if the soldiers were civilians instead.[109]

It is worth remembering that most military expenditures are, overall, a drag on the economy. Bombs and military aircraft are sunk costs, with little or no contribution to productivity. In wartime, there is massive destruction of buildings, factories and the like. During wars, governments typically finance military operations through massive expansion of debt. Another factor is the large amount of waste and corruption involved in military operations.

Historians of technology note that many worthwhile inventions come

107 Stephen Zunes, "The role of non-violent action in the downfall of apartheid," *Journal of Modern African Studies,* vol. 37, 1999, pp. 137–169.

108 Richard Hengeveld and Jaap Rodenburg (editors), *Embargo: Apartheid's Oil secrets Revealed* (Amsterdam: Amsterdam University Press, 1995).

109 Militaries might provide special deals to farmers, with inflated prices to increase their income. This involves an additional drain on the economy.

out of military research. However, if the same urgent investment were put into civilian research, quite likely the return would be even greater.

All this is to say that there is no automatic connection between businesses and militaries. If governments offer opportunities for making profit, then some businesses will pursue them, so if governments funded bicycle networks rather than missiles, businesses would adapt.

The youth movement

It is usually inaccurate to speak of a social movement composed of or on behalf of youth. However, it is certainly true that young people have often been at the forefront of protest and social change. In campaigns to challenge longstanding traditions, youth are often prominent, in part because they have less stake in tradition and in part because the traditions may be blocking social advancement. In numerous countries, university students have led protests against governments, including against repressive measures. Young people were the leaders of the Serbian group Otpor that led the struggle that toppled ruler Slobodan Milošević in 2000. Note that movements are not necessarily progressive: youth are prominent among skinhead groups that attack gays and racial minorities.

Given the willingness of many young people to take action and, in many cases, to take risky actions, there is a special role for them in social defence: leading front-line protests that involve physical danger. In general, methods of nonviolent action are effective in part because they allow widespread participation. Nonetheless, some nonviolent actions require special types of physical skills and mental capacities. Examples abound in environmental and peace campaigning, for example altering billboards on the sides of buildings and taking small craft in front of nuclear ships.

In nonviolent resistance, no one should be pressured to undertake dangerous tasks, especially given that dispersed tactics such as strikes and boycotts are available and very powerful. Nevertheless, when individuals

119

volunteer for risky roles, it may be appropriate to include them in a resistance campaign. When youth have great passion and willingness to take a stand, then including them in risky roles takes advantage of their capacities. Their courage can be inspirational for others.

At the moment, the special ways that youth might be integrated into social defence remain speculative. The main thing now is to include them as equals in planning and in actual struggles.

Faith-based movements

Faith based movements and organisations have played an important role in some cases of non-armed political revolutions in recent decades. The Catholic Church played a crucial role in the unarmed transformations of several countries including Poland, Philippines and Chile. In 1978, Karol Wojtyla, archbishop of Krakow, was elected as the first Polish pope: John Paul II. His moral support for the Solidarity movement that was challenging the communist dictatorship in Poland was visible when he visited the country and held huge meetings and masses.

In 1978 when Pope John Paul II stood on the balcony of St. Peter's, he said, "Be not afraid," and in closing prayed, "Let the Spirit descend. Let the Spirit descend, and renew the face of the earth, the face of this land." While this prayer and exhortation were said to the world, the Polish people, especially, knew he was addressing them. Solidarity leader Lech Wałęsa said that these words energised the movement in Poland. At the same time, Yuri Andropov, then head of the KGB, the Soviet secret police, commenced a study of the implications of a Polish pope, concluding that this papacy would destabilise Poland and undermine Soviet authority in the communist bloc.

On 5 June 1979, Pope John Paul II arrived in Poland to visit his homeland. As he descended the stairs of the plane in Warsaw, he kissed the ground and incited a spiritual earthquake. During his visit at the Auschwitz concentration camp, the symbol of the evil of totalitarianism, he told the thousands of people gathered from the Eastern European countries to resist the falsehoods they had been told: "You are not who they say you are, so let me remind you who you are."[110] What was done by the church behind the scenes will not be known in detail until a whistleblower within the Vatican gives us access to the secret files. There are indications that the church played a crucial role.[111]

There are many other examples. In Norway under the Nazi occupation during World War II, the State Church played an important role in the civil resistance. Priests functioned as couriers and provided moral support in difficult situations. Both in Vietnam and Burma, Buddhist monks played a crucial role in the struggle against tyrants. The Catholic church played an important role in the uprising against President Ferdinand Marcos in the Philippines in 1986.

In Egypt, the Muslim Brotherhood played a constructive role in the overthrow of dictator Hosni Mubarak in 2011. The Brotherhood had the capacities and organisational skills to organise the weeks-long vigils on central squares in the cities.

On the surface, it might seem that faith-based movements provide no particular skills or leverage to resist aggression and repression. What they provide, potentially, is belief and solidarity. Some individuals are willing to make incredible sacrifices for their religious beliefs.

Highly repressive governments commonly try to crush any groups that could offer a platform for organising resistance, including political parties, trade unions and non-government organisations. Religious groups, because they tap deep-seated personal commitments, sometimes become the primary basis for resistance, as in the case of liberation theology in the face of dictatorships in South America.

On the other hand, churches and religious leaders often back the status quo, and endorse or are complicit with militarism and war. Faith-based movements are not guaranteed to help nonviolent resisters.

The implications for a social defence system are not clear. Those who want to promote social defence should be aware of the role of faith and

---

110 Catholic Straight Answers, "What was Pope John Paul II's role in the fall of the Soviet Union?" http://catholicstraightanswers.com/pope-john-paul-iis-role-fall-soviet-union/

111 Ronald C. Monticone, *The Catholic Church in Communist Poland, 1945–1985: Forty Years of Church-state Relations* (New York: East European Monographs, 1986).

organised religion in their own societies and in possible aggressors. There is much more to learn about the relationship between faith and social defence.

The peace movement

The peace movement is the most obvious host for promoting social defence because, after all, social defence, if implemented worldwide, eliminates the threat of war. However, for most of its history, the peace movement has been more focused on opposing war than on promoting alternatives to military systems. It might better be labelled the anti-war movement.

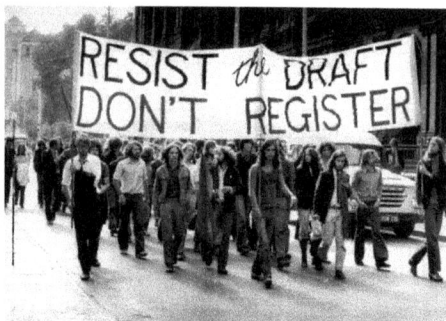

The peace movement has been responsible for numerous important changes: preventing wars, bringing wars to an end, opposing military races, hindering military operations, and banning or stigmatising particular types of weapons, including nuclear weapons, chemical weapons and land mines. Although it can be difficult to assign responsibility for prevention, the movement against nuclear weapons has been vital in restraining nuclear arms races and probably therefore in preventing nuclear war.[112]

The peace movement, like most social movements, is not a single entity, but is composed of a variety of organisations, campaigns, and members with a diversity of viewpoints. Much anti-war campaigning is reactive, emerging in response to major developments. In the late 1950s, protest campaigns developed against nuclear weapons, in part as a response to above-ground testing of nuclear explosives with resulting radioactive fallout. Then, after the passing of the partial atmospheric nuclear test ban treaty in 1963, the movement rapidly declined. It re-emerged in the late 1970s and early 1980s, even larger and stronger, in response to the placing of US nuclear weapons in Western Europe. The movement was highly influential but, after the end of the Cold War at the end of the 1980s, again declined to near invisibility.

---

112 Lawrence S. Wittner, *The Struggle against the Bomb*, three volumes (Stanford, CA: Stanford UP, 1993–2003).

During the Cold War, the Soviet Union and satellite states in Eastern Europe set up official peace organisations. These government-sponsored groups provided a lot of rhetoric in favour of peace but in practice were only concerned with militarism in the West: they were tools of Soviet foreign policy. This was obvious enough within the Soviet bloc, and tainted the word "peace" for many years. In many Western countries, pro-Soviet or pro-Communist groups joined peace movements and helped make them focus on opposing capitalist militarism.

So far, Communist and Marxist groups have shown little interest in social defence. More commonly, they support armed struggle against capitalist states and capitalist militaries. The traditional Leninist strategy is for a party representing the working class to capture state power and then to use the power of the state to smash capitalism and introduce socialism. This all assumed continuation of the military, under control of Marxist leaders.

The views of many Marxists are far more sophisticated than this, but often with the same underlying assumption about military forces: they are to be retained in service of the people. As a result, few Marxists have been enthusiasts for social defence. Instead, in their support for armed struggle, some of them are unsympathetic or even hostile to nonviolent action.

Another important inspiration within Western peace groups has been pacifism, which involves individual refusal to participate in militaries and collective opposition to all wars. The usual demand made of governments was disarmament: dismantling weapons systems, closing military bases and reducing the size of military forces. However, the demand for disarmament has always been vulnerable to the charge that it will leave a country defenceless. There have been proponents of unilateral nuclear disarmament, but they have seldom been able to shape policy. The result is that disarmament is normally seen as a mutual process, with governments entering negotiations to reduce their arsenals. However, when disarmament becomes a matter of government negotiations, the peace movement is sidelined, becoming mainly a pressure group.

Some pacifists in the past saw the ideal society as one without conflict. This meant they were unsympathetic to social defence, which assumes the continuation of conflict, waged through nonviolent rather than violent means. Gene Sharp developed his model of nonviolent action in part through encounters with these sorts of pacifists. Today, there may not be so many pacifists who seek a world without conflict.

When peace movements surge in strength, many people join who have no particular commitments to Marxism, pacifism or other belief systems, except that they oppose military preparations or wars. The massive mobilisation in 2003 against the impending invasion of Iraq is an example. All sorts of people attended rallies, with their primary concern to oppose an unnecessary war. Few of them would have even heard of social defence.

Probably the most common belief underlying such anti-war mobilisations is that society can remain much the same as it is today, except that aggressive war can be prevented. The movement against nuclear weapons pushed for reduction and eventually elimination of nuclear arsenals, but leaving militaries otherwise unchanged. Campaigners did not offer visions beyond this, in part because of the stigma attached to "unilateral disarmament." Many pushing for nuclear disarmament imagined a gradual reduction of offensive weapons: first nuclear weapons, then others later on.

In summary, few participants in peace movements have pursued nonviolent alternatives to the military. Marxists have opposed capitalist militarism, endorsing armed struggle for liberation. Pacifists have opposed all wars, but most commonly through individual withdrawal rather than developing collective alternatives. Many participants in mass mobilisations against particular wars or types of weapons have not envisaged a long-term struggle to develop alternatives to military forces, and have not looked beyond the end of wars or the elimination of weapons such as chemical weapons or land mines.

As noted in chapter 1, during the 1980s there were activist groups in several countries pursuing social defence. Most of these groups grew out of the peace movement. But with the end of the cold war, interest in alternatives declined. The peace movement was a stimulus for thinking about social defence, but when the movement shrunk, this stimulus nearly disappeared.

Global justice movement

In the 1990s, a new sort of social movement emerged. In the media, it has usually been called the antiglobalisation movement, but it is primarily against corporate globalisation and in particular against all the processes leading to greater economic and social inequality. This new movement has been called the global justice movement or sometimes the movement of movements. It incorporates feminist, environmental, labour and other agendas, all in support of greater equality and direct participation in decision-making.

The goals of the peace movement fit naturally in the global justice movement, because militaries prop up the system of states and corporations that is driving inequality and subordination of citizens. Just as importantly, the movement of movements is largely committed to nonviolent means of social change, often in the spirit of "the means of change should reflect the goals." The global justice movement has been inspired by campaigns for local autonomy, for example the Zapatistas in Chiapas, Mexico.

The movement seems to be an ideal home or umbrella for efforts towards social defence. So why has social defence been such a low profile within the movement? Part of the explanation is the so-called war on terror in the aftermath of 9/11. The war on terror has involved a mobilisation of military and state security forces to serve state power, with the pretext being to combat a foe that, in considerable part, has been manufactured and fostered by the war on terror itself. Alternative approaches to combatting terrorism have been sidelined. More importantly, the war on terror sets the agenda: terrorism is the central focus. Along the way, social defence has been marginalised.

Social defence is a natural component of the global justice movement. By thinking in terms of how a community can defend itself from aggression and repression, and by taking steps to foster skills and preparation for such a defence, communities are empowered. They can use their skills and preparation to challenge various forms of oppression associated with corporate globalisation.

This sort of connection was quite clear in the Occupy movement. Many Occupy groups trained in and used methods of cooperative decision-making, mutual help and nonviolent action. To expand the use of these methods, social defence provides a guide.

Conclusion

Social movements are the most promising basis for promoting social defence, and social defence provides a framework for building a resilient, self-governing community. As well as the movements we've discussed here, there are others that could make a contribution to social defence, for example animal liberation, anti-racism, queer, and disability rights. Not every movement has potential commonalities with social defence. Those that pursue greater equality and justice have the strongest connections, because equality and justice make a society worth defending.

There are two key differences between military defence and social defence. Most obviously, the methods used in social defence do not involve physical violence. The other difference is in participation: social defence requires support from most people, and participation by a large number. For the same reason, the most promising way to move towards social defence is to use nonviolent methods and to work through social movements that have a participatory ethos.

7
What you can do

If you want to help move from military systems to social defence, what can you do? This question is not easy to answer, because you have your own knowledge and skills and live in your own circumstances. A teenage athlete has a different set of skills than a retired librarian, and a soldier is in a different situation than a farmer. What we do here is describe some possible actions for different sorts of people in the hope that these might give ideas that are relevant.

We list quite a few possibilities here, but no one could be expected to do very many of them. Often it is better to do one thing well rather than do lots of things less well. It all depends on the person and the circumstances.[113]

Have conversations

Talking to people about social defence can be very useful. There are various ways to approach this. One is to say, "Imagine that the government declares martial law and arrests anyone who seems like a threat. What could we do to resist, without using violence?" You can be ready with some ideas about what you might do yourself, such as sending messages to friends in other countries, talking to neighbours, setting up an online resistance group or organising a rally. You could come prepared with suggestions for protests, boycotts or strikes. But the main thing is to encourage people to think about what they could do, using their own knowledge, skills and networks.

Because social defence is not widely known or understood, it is useful to introduce relevant ideas. You don't even need to use terms like "social defence." The main thing is to get people thinking about what *they* could do.

---

113 For other ideas, see Jacki Quilty, Lynne Dickins, Phil Anderson and Brian Martin. *Capital Defence: Social Defence for Canberra* (Canberra: Canberra Peacemakers, 1986); Brian Martin, "Social defence: arguments and actions," in Shelley Anderson and Janet Larmore (eds.), *Nonviolent Struggle and Social Defence* (London: War Resisters' International and the Myrtle Solomon Memorial Fund Subcommittee, 1991), pp. 81–141.

Join action groups

Joining an action group often provides a useful connection to promoting social defence. There are various possibilities: peace groups, feminist groups, environmental groups and many others. The most relevant sort of group is one involved in nonviolent actions or social change at the grassroots.

For example, a climate change group that organises protests at major greenhouse gas producers or helps neighbourhoods develop local energy self-reliance is ideal. It offers skills useful for resisting repression (organising protests, boycotts, strikes) or useful for building an energy system that is less vulnerable to a hostile takeover. In such a group, you can learn skills, gain understanding and build networks.

Less directly relevant are groups oriented to lobbying and influencing politicians. If the politicians are the problem, or are replaced by ones who are, this approach offers less protection.

Being in a group, even one without an obvious connection to social defence, can help build networks. If there is a threat, to you personally or to society, cross-cutting horizontal networks are important. It means you can connect with other people, with different skills and leverage, for example lawyers, computer specialists and bus drivers.

Another value in being involved in an action group is developing skills for operating in a group. This might sound easy but often it's not. People have different personalities, jobs, worries, relationships and obligations. Working together inevitably involves interacting and negotiating with others, taking into account their personal strengths and weaknesses. Ideally it means helping them develop as capable and responsible individuals. All this is relevant to social defence. When people are skilled in dealing with their own emotions and the emotions of others, they are better able to act effectively in a crisis.

Being in a group can be a stimulating experience. It involves learning, engaging relationships and the satisfaction of working together. However, some groups are subject to power plays, toxic behaviours and even abuse.

128

If you are skilled at dealing with such problems, you can treat this as a challenge. If not, it's probably better to leave and find a better place to put your energies.

Ideally, being an activist should be fun. Groups should reflect the sort of society they are seeking to create.

Improve online skills

Navigating online is part of everyday life in ever more ways. Lots of people walk around staring at their screens or texting. Online activity is also important in emergencies, and in social defence.

In defending against aggression and repression, it is vital for resisters to be able to communicate with each other, to share information and coordinate actions. Communicating with opponents is valuable too, to win them over or negotiate. You can do various things to improve your capacity to communicate in an emergency.

First there is preparation. There are people you will want to contact in a crisis. What will you do if your phone is lost, disabled or taken over? Do you have crucial information backed up? If you try to contact someone important to you – family member, friend or activist – and they don't answer, what do you do? Do you have an alternative way to contact them? What if someone has taken over their phone and is extracting information from it? You need to think of contingencies, think how you will overcome obstacles and make preparations accordingly.

Second there is practice. Your preparations might be good or not so good, but you won't know until they are tested. You can try out various scenarios, such as pretending to lose your phone and seeing how quickly you can recover (for example by getting another phone and downloading crucial information from your backup location).

Improve online security

Social media enable surveillance. If an enemy or repressive government has access to all the information collected about digital activities – for example bank transactions and phone calls – they can use this to identify resisters, track them, anticipate their actions, arrest them or even kill them.

A social defence system would involve designing communication systems so no hostile authorities would have access to this sort of surveillance capacity. However, at the moment the best that most individuals can do is to make their own communications as secure as possible. This includes learning how to use encryption, using social media platforms that do not save or share personal data, using secure web browsers, and not carrying trackable devices when having sensitive conversations.

Use your online network

An important skill is being able to network, in particular to help organise actions. You have a set of contacts online. Which of them would sign a petition? Which of them would attend an online meeting? Which of them would join a boycott? How would you approach them?

If one of your contacts made a request to join an action, would you refuse, not respond, join the action, and/or encourage others to join it? How would you make your decision? Is trust crucial? What about checking beforehand to be sure the request is based on correct information? How much assurance do you need before you commit yourself? What are the risks if you do?

Many people have lots of contacts. Some are strong connections, to people you know well. Others are "weak," to people you don't know very well. Strong connections are important, but so are weak ones, depending on the circumstances. The key is knowing how to work with your connections.

Every day, you probably obtain information from many different sources, including messages from friends, news stories (from mass media, Facebook, etc.), advertising and Wikipedia. It is a crucially important skill to be able to determine how reliable information is. Stories that are wrong or misleading sometimes spread like wildfire. You need to be able to figure out which stories are accurate, which are important, and what to do with the information.

Because there is so much information available, trying to figure out accuracy, importance and implications is very difficult when you're on your own. Getting together with several others can be valuable. The group can practise analysing breaking news and trying to determine, as soon as possible, whether it is credible. You can also practise delving behind the news, to stories that receive little attention but are important. You can attend protests and compare your direct observations to online reports.

The online environment has huge potential, but there are many pitfalls. By becoming an astute navigator, and coordinating with others, you can become skilled in information politics. This is crucially important in defending against aggression and repression.

Learn how people think and behave

Being able to understand people's behaviour is a really useful skill. Some people have an intuitive sense of what others are thinking, but whatever your skill level, it can be improved by observation and study.

It's useful to know who can be relied on, especially in an emergency, and who will fail to deliver. It's useful to know who tries to dominate others and know how to resist their attempts. It's useful to know who is selfish and who tries to curry favour with authorities. It's useful to know who thinks independently and usually behaves in a principled way.

This sort of knowledge of people's psychology is useful in everyday life, including at home, school, the workplace and voluntary groups. It is also crucial in social defence. Faced by an emergency, faced by repressive police and by attempts to divide and rule, figuring out what people will do is vitally important. It's important to remember that many people behave differently when under pressure.

To improve your understanding, a first step is to pay attention to what people say and what they do. Some people are more self-centred than others; some are outspoken; some gossip continually; some are reserved and steady; some are burning with resentment.

A second step is to interact with people and learn from the interactions. You can see how they react to compliments and criticisms, to requests and favours. You can notice how they pay attention when you're speaking. You can mention some gossip and see whether they pass it on. You can entrust them with some personal information and see whether they maintain confidentiality.

A third step is to learn from studies of human behaviour.[114] Studies show that most people lie regularly – they tell falsehoods and do not reveal

---

114 A valuable treatment is Nicholas Epley, *Mindwise: How We Understand What Others Think, Believe, Feel and Want* (London: Penguin, 2014).

131

truths. In many cases, lies are intended to help others, such as when you say nice things about someone's appearance. The most dangerous lies are ones told by authorities that cause harm.[115]

You can learn about the two-minds model, the idea that people seem to have two different ways of mental processing. One is rapid, automatic and usually unconscious. This intuitive mind often shapes people's gut reactions and immediate impressions. The second mind is slow, requires more effort and is usually conscious. This rational mind is good for making careful judgements.[116]

Brian has often had a disconcerting experience when talking with others about social defence. When someone raises an objection, for example that violence will always triumph over nonviolence, he gives examples and refers to research findings showing this is false. But for some individuals it doesn't seem to matter what he says: they continue to be sceptical. This can be interpreted as their intuitive mind taking over, telling them that this idea is wrong or dangerous. Their rational mind then tries to come up with plausible-sounding objections. We can deal with the objections but not so easily with the gut reaction.

The most important thing you can do is to try to understand your own psychology. You can observe your thoughts and behaviour and see how they relate to each other. You can also ask others to provide candid feedback on what you say and do. Self-understanding is vital, especially in an emergency. It is also very difficult to achieve. Self-deception is common.[117] Some self-deception is functional, such as having hope for success even when prospects are poor, because it makes us willing to keep trying. But other types of self-deception are damaging, such as trusting in leaders who continually betray their followers. Self-understanding is a counter to the inducements by governments to serve their interests.

---

115 On lying and activism, see Brian Martin, *The Deceptive Activist* (Sparsnäs, Sweden: Irene Publishing, 2017).

116 For an accessible and insightful treatment of the two minds, see Jonathan Haidt, *The Righteous Mind: Why Good People Are Divided by Politics and Religion* (New York: Pantheon, 2012). See also Daniel Kahneman, *Thinking, Fast and Slow* (New York: Farrar, Straus and Giroux, 2011).

117 Robert Trivers, *The Folly of Fools: The Logic of Deceit and Self-Deception in Human Life* (New York: Basic Books, 2011).

Run an exercise

Think of people who might be willing to join you in an exercise in emergency preparedness. They could be relatives, neighbours, work mates, friends or members of an action group. It might be three of you or up to a dozen or more. It's probably best to start with a small group to see what happens and then move to larger groups.

You can work with the group members to prepare for contingencies. You might think of a danger needing an immediate, coordinated response: a fire, a robbery, a group member who is injured or arrested, stalking of a group member or a threat to reveal private information (blackmail). The closer the danger is to something that might actually affect group members, the better.

Preparation might be discussing who would contact whom, who would take responsibility, how information would be verified, how decisions would be made, what other people might be contacted, who has relevant skills (medical, communication, etc.) and anything else relevant.

The actual exercise is a simulation, which is like a fire drill. You do everything you would do in an actual emergency, with some code to ensure everyone knows it's just a practice run. If you have experience with dress rehearsals or military exercises, you will have ideas about how to do this. You might arrange for someone to decide the scenario and to begin the exercise by sending a message. Then you do the simulation. It might last only a few minutes, depending on what's involved. Afterwards, you discuss what happened. Did communication operate as planned? Were there unanticipated problems? How can we better prepare?

Exercises are extremely valuable in helping people become used to taking responsibility in a crisis. If you find that everything operates smoothly, then you can choose a more challenging scenario. You can even try to make it more interesting by having rewards and a celebration.

Develop cultural skills

Suppose, where you live, people fear invasion from a foreign power. In Australia, some people fear an invasion from Indonesia. Others worry more about China, Russia, Vietnam or the United States. Sometimes these fears are unrealistic. Regardless of the actual threat, a social defence system benefits from many people being knowledgeable about the culture in foreign countries from which threats are feared.

A culture involves language, traditions, rituals and beliefs. The more you know about the foreign culture, the better able you are to take action against any actual threat and, if there is no actual threat, the better able you are to reassure others who are afraid.

Imagine there is an actual threat of an invasion from another country. A powerful way to counter this threat is to build alliances with citizen groups in that country, in particular groups that would oppose an invasion. In the case of Australia and Indonesia, this would mean Australians building alliances with citizen groups in Indonesia. To do this, it helps to know the Indonesian language, to understand Indonesian history and traditions, and to know how to interact with Indonesian people, including soldiers.

If there is no actual threat, then a different task may be more important: informing people in your own country about what Indonesians are actually thinking and doing. To contribute to this, you can write articles, produce podcasts, create artwork, and set up cultural exchanges. The more that ordinary Australians and Indonesians know about each other, the more likely they are to oppose any aggression instigated by their governments and the less likely they are to be susceptible to fear-mongering by their governments about foreign threats.

It can be helpful to work on cultural skills with a group of friends. If you can find a group in a foreign country to work with, this is even better.

Learn to fraternise

A powerful technique of resistance is to communicate with aggressors and reduce their commitment. With the right sort of dialogue, some of them might become less aggressive and more sympathetic to your cause, or even serve your cause by defecting or by feeding information about the aggression.

In the case of a foreign invasion or occupation, fraternisation involves talking with enemy soldiers, as in Czechoslovakia 1968. In the case of a military coup or a repressive government, fraternisation involves talking with police and troops in your own country.

To fraternise more effectively, learning and practice are vital. This might be learning a foreign language or learning about the way that police and soldiers are trained, what their daily lives are like, what they believe and what values they hold. To communicate effectively, it is always important to know your audience.

what are other words for fraternise?

fraternize, associate, socialise, hobnob, join, consort, socialize, mix, associate with, keep company

If you have some friends who work in the police or army, you can talk to them about what they do in their work, about their complaints and concerns, and about how they see protesters. The more you understand how they think, the better able you will be to communicate your message.

Practice is crucial. You have something you want to say and you know something about the person you want to say it to. So try it out, see what happens and learn from the response. If you have a friend in the police or army, you might be able to get them to agree to let you practise with them, or with some of their colleagues.

There are all sorts of scenarios to consider. Maybe you will be able to talk one-on-one with a soldier. If you are at a rally and police are in a line behind helmets and shields, it is more difficult to communicate. If you are exchanging texts with a soldier, different techniques might be suitable.

Fraternisation is not always effective, and not necessarily the best strategy. Sometimes it is better to use the technique of ostracism, which means refusing to interact with others. If soldiers come to buy some goods, you turn away and refuse to speak with them. This method has been used in some resistance situations.

By learning beforehand about how possible aggressors think and respond, you are better able to judge whether fraternisation or ostracism, or some other technique, is better. Sometimes the chosen approach should be used for all opposition forces. At other times, different approaches for different individuals might be better.

If your preparations for fraternisation are advanced, you can even run experiments to compare different methods. You and others try out different arguments or styles of speaking with different troops and see which ones work best.[118]

Develop transition plans

Changing from military defence to social defence could happen suddenly, for example as a result of a crisis. In Czechoslovakia in 1968, military defence wasn't used against the Soviet invasion.[119] If the spontaneous nonviolent resistance had been successful in the long term, then this might have provided a motivation to get rid of military forces and rely entirely on unarmed methods.

Another possibility is that the transition from military to social defence could happen gradually, according to a careful plan.

In either case, it is worthwhile to have transition plans. Even if they are never used, plans can be helpful in reducing fears about change, especially fears by soldiers and workers in arms production about loss of their jobs.

A transition plan needs to address several things. For ending reliance on military methods, it needs to include changing military production to production for human needs. It needs to include alternative jobs for military personnel. It needs to cover military-oriented infrastructure such as airports, communication systems and surveillance. It needs to address military-oriented education, advertising, memorials and art. It needs to do all this with great sensitivity to the concerns of those involved.

The other side of a transition plan is building the capacity for nonviolent deterrence and resistance. We've addressed this in other parts of this book.

During the Cold War, campaigners linked to the peace movement pushed for what is called peace conversion or economic conversion. This means converting factories that produce military goods and services so that they produce, instead, goods and services for civilian purposes. In some cases this is straightforward. A shipbuilding facility can shift from producing military vessels to civilian vessels. But some military facilities are highly specialised, so it is difficult to convert them.

A powerful option is to let workers decide how to convert their operations. In the 1970s, workers at Lucas Aerospace in Britain took the initiative to

---

118 Brian Martin and Majken Jul Sørensen, "Investigating nonviolent action by experimental testing," *Journal of Resistance Studies*, vol. 3, no. 2, 2017, pp. 42–65.

119 See chapter 3.

propose alternative products drawing on their skills and equipment.[120] What this experience showed was that workers, if given the opportunity to help decide what to produce and how to produce it, were attuned to the needs of the community.

A transition plan also needs to include getting rid of military equipment, everything from nuclear missiles to rifles and bullets. Care is needed to avoid environmental damage. Some of the best-informed people to help develop and carry out such plans are military personnel.

Developing a transition plan is not an easy task. It requires gathering information, consulting with a wide range of people, and winning over military personnel to the feasibility of the plan. Rather than seeing a transition plan as a blueprint, it may be better to see it as part of the process of raising awareness about social defence and how it could be implemented. A sensible plan is also useful if there is a crisis providing an opportunity to make a change.

---

120 See the discussion in chapter 6.

8
Kynnefjäll:
Local people versus the nuclear industry

The idea of social defence is to develop the capacity of citizens to use nonviolent methods to deter and defend against aggression and repression, enabling militaries to be phased out. But this will not happen quickly. Meanwhile, campaigners have been using nonviolent action for decades, which means there's much that advocates of social defence can learn from nonviolent campaigns. Here we describe one particular campaign and then say how it relates to promoting the capacity for social defence.

Late in the 1940s, the early nuclear industry in Sweden had a huge advantage compared to most other states in Europe. Because Sweden had not been directly involved in WWII, its industry and infrastructure were intact and both the military and business elites saw possibilities to utilise energy from nuclear fission. Within the military establishment, plans for a nuclear bomb moved from an idea to practical research and development. The first research program was an offshoot from military research and in 1947 the semi-civil Atomic Energy Company was established. In 1954 the first heavy water research reactor (R1) was built on the campus of the Swedish Technical University in Stockholm. Under the cover of civilian research, the main purpose was to build a Swedish nuclear bomb.[121] By 1964, one more reactor (R2) was in operation in Studsvik. A third reactor in Marviken was finished but due to security issues never started. The plant was converted to an oil-fuelled power station, humorously called the only oil-fired nuclear power station in the world.

Sweden had its own uranium resources and the government planned for huge mining projects. These became very controversial due to the environmental impacts. For the planned production of the 60 nuclear bombs, the uranium should be processed to plutonium. AB Atomenergi

---

121 "NRC seeking more information about 1972 Swedish plutonium tests," *Nucleonics Week*, vol. 26, no. 19, 1985, pp. 1–2; Wilhelm Agrell, *Svenska förintelsevapen: utvecklingen av kemiska och nukleära stridsmedel 1928-1970* (Lund: Historiska Media, 2002).

planned a factory for this in the Sannäs fjord in Tanum municipality.[122]

In 1960, the Swedish military, without the knowledge of Parliament, made a secret contract with a company called AB Atomenergi (later renamed Studsvik Energiteknik AB) to develop and operate a plutonium reprocessing plant. The company chose to locate the plant near Sannäs, as far from the Baltic Sea as possible. There, caves could be excavated in the stone cliffs to hide the operation. In 1963 AB Atomenergi made its first purchase of land in the Sannäs area, which was eventually expanded to 230 hectares in 1966. A major portion of the money to buy this land came directly from the Swedish military.[123]

Years of strong local protests resulted in the plans being cancelled. The plans for a bomb continued and were not cancelled until the early 1970s. Political pressure and protests made the plans impossible to implement and officially the development ended. There are indications that part of the research continued for years after the parliament had decided to stop the R&D.

Despite a lot of protest, the government continued to build nuclear power stations. In 1980 the parliament decided to hold a referendum on the issue. In a political scam, the majority in the parliament decided that there should be three options to vote for in the referendum.[124] In this way

---

122 Å. Hultgren, *The Reprocessing of Nuclear Fuel. Summary of a report to the Swedish government from a working party representing the ministries of industry, agriculture, and physical planning and local government* (Stockholm: AB Atomenergi, 1971).

123 Marianne Lindström, Karl-Inge Åhäll, Olov Holmstrand, Björn Helander, and Miles Goldstick, "Nuclear waste in Sweden – the problem is not solved!" *Nonuclear. se: Environmental Views on Energy,* June 1988.

124 The options:
1. Nuclear power would be phased out over a period that would not impact too severely on employment and welfare. The twelve nuclear power stations operating or under construction would continue to be used until renewable sources became available, in order to reduce dependence on oil. There would also be no further expansion of nuclear power and the order in which the existing nuclear power stations would close down would be dependent on security.
2. As with proposal 1, but efforts would also be made to reduce energy consumption whilst protecting low income groups, including phasing out electric heating and

they made sure that none of the alternatives got 50% or more of the votes and it was left to the Parliament to interpret the result. The result was that all planned reactors were built. The well-organised campaign for the third option – to halt expansion of nuclear power – included a wide variety of environmental groups, political parties and the peace movement.

The main issue after the referendum become what to do with the waste. In order to load the remaining planned reactors, the authorities promised to find a safe storage location for all the waste. For leading politicians as well as the nuclear industry, finding a safe storage became crucial in order to gain necessary support for expanding the number of reactors. Waste storage became the main focus for the opposition to nuclear power.

One of the most attractive places for nuclear waste storage was the mountain Kynnefjäll on the Swedish west coast. It was sparsely populated

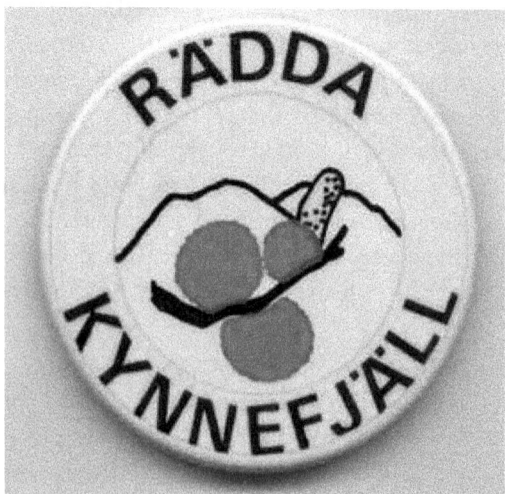

and accessible with cars, huge ships, and railway. This was important since the transportation from the reactors to the storage was a problematic part of the waste chain. The industry wanted all options for how get the waste to the final storage. Kynnefjäll is located half an hour by car from the site for the planned plutonium factory in Sannäs. The

increased R&D of renewable energy led by the government. In addition, a security committee with local membership would be put in place at each nuclear power plant and the public sector would take responsibility for generating and distributing electricity. Nuclear power plants would be owned by central and local government and any surplus profits from hydroelectric generation would be subject to a 100% tax rate.

3. The expansion of nuclear power would cease immediately and the six operational stations would be subject to stricter conditions and closed within ten years. Efforts would be made to reduce energy consumption and to increase renewable energy capacity. Uranium mining would be banned and efforts to prevent the proliferation of nuclear weapons would be enhanced.

opposition from the 1970s played a role when opposition to the storage started. Some of those who took part in the successful campaign against the "bomb factory" in the 1970s were engaged also at Kynnefjäll. Another factor that played a role in the mobilising against the storage was the fact that this part of Sweden had the highest percentage of the population opposing all forms of nuclear power. This was seen in the referendum in 1980 and in opinion polls. From this perspective it was not a wise decision by the industry to place the planned storage in this part of the country; the locals did not appreciate nuclear facilities of any sort and they had experience in successfully opposing unwelcome developments.

When the plans for "test drilling" at Kynnefjäll become known to the public, local people started to discuss how to react. Local farmers, environmental activists, trade unionists and other concerned citizens made the first plans on how to stop the drilling. The main idea was to place their own bodies in front of the machinery.

In April 1980, before the plans were finalised and people ready to act, drilling equipment suddenly were spotted along one of the few roads leading up to the planned site for the first drilling hole. Since the construction machinery was heavy and the dirt roads in bad condition, they were bogged down early on the first day. When local people saw this, they immediately called for a 24–7 blockade of the road. People came and stayed in tents and caravans overnight. After a chaotic start, it soon developed into a pretty well organised campaign.

The three roads leading up to the drilling site were put under observation and a telephone chain established to call for more people to join as soon as police or drilling equipment were observed approaching. The blockade made it to the local and regional media and as the summer approached more and more people joined the campaign. Plans were made for a march and the small tent and caravan camp was moved up to the actual drilling site. Discussions and speculations on how to act in different scenarios become the main focus for all activists.

Anyone who has experienced an early phase of such campaigns will not be surprised that gossip, rumours, theories and nerves were pretty intense. Strong motivations combined with limited factual information made the "activist aura" stressful for many, especially the inexperienced. Every small piece of information, whether from the media or from "friends of friends," was discussed, stripped down and combined with other elements of what

141

was regarded as knowledge. Despite strong personalities and some level of disagreement, the outcome in this case was a high level of consensus on how to move on.

One factor that should not be underestimated was the number of resolute and stalwart farmers with self-confidence. Their wisdom made a difference in the decision making process.

According to paragraph 136a of the Swedish Law of Housing, dating from the 1960s, municipalities had veto power over activities that they decided were unacceptable. But the local veto did not cover all types of environmentally hazardous activities, for example test drilling for a high-level nuclear waste storage facility. At Kynnefjäll the plans were to test whether the stones were of sufficient quality to store spent fuel from nuclear reactors. However, the Government can rule that any activity falls under the veto law. But the majority in the Parliament eagerly supported the search for suitable storage and had no intention of stopping the test drilling.

At the local level, all three municipalities around Kynnefjäll – Tanum, Munkedal and Ed – opposed the plans. This local support came to play an important role for the campaign in the years ahead. It was taken for granted that if the planned test drilling showed that the mountain was suitable for storing waste, it would be extremely difficult to prevent plans for actual storage. In 1987 the Swedish National Council for Nuclear Waste (SKN) requested that the Government weaken the local veto.

It was obvious that this could be a long struggle. Plans were made by the activists for a sustained vigil combined with an effective telephone chain and mobilisation of more people every summer. From early on they wanted to have at least two people in the vigil 24–7 and ready to alert others if needed. During the first summer it become clear that SKB (Svensk Kärnbränslehantering), the company responsible for the drilling, was not in a hurry and was not interested in confrontations with local people. Their strategy was to wait until the activists lost interest and left the site.

But the campaign had no plans to end soon and applied to local authorities for permission to build a cabin for the vigil. The building permit was given and a nice red cabin was built close to the planned first drilling. That made it more comfortable to stay on guard day and night in the long dark autumn and the cold winter nights. It was decided to have a minimum of two people present at all times. They worked in 12-hour shifts, from 6am to 6pm and 6pm to 6am. Often there were more people present and

in the weekends the cabin become a popular place to visit for people in the region. As media coverage grew, people from all over the country started to sign up for a shift in the cabin. Later the campaign also had visitors from many countries around the world.

The campaign agreed from day one that this should be a completely nonviolent campaign. A few voices in favour of using sabotage, like putting sugar in the fuel tanks of construction machinery, were resolutely opposed. In some years, activists organised small-scale nonviolence trainings to prepare for civil disobedience and confrontations with the police. But the preparations mainly involved talking through how to behave in different scenarios. The core of the strategy was to use their bodies to prevent construction machinery from being used.

When the first actions started in April 1980 none of the activists could imagine the duration of this vigil and the other actions that accompanied it. The views among activists and supporters were that this could take some time and that it was important to make the campaign sustainable: to be prepared for a long struggle. As always there were those among the activists who told journalists: "We will never give up." Representatives from SKB smiled at such comments. They too were aware that it could take some time. The storage of the waste had some temporary solutions and the final solution could wait years and even decades. It was taken for granted that the activists would eventually give up.

In the years that followed, the vigil continued every day and night. The majority of those who took 12-hour shifts were local people: farmers, fishermen, housewives, teachers and students. When Greenpeace arrived with its professional activists, they were invited to take a 12-hour shift or two, but were not invited to sit on the steering committee. In hindsight this was a wise decision. To keep the campaign based on local resources made the struggle more sustainable. The key activists were fighting for their own society, for the future of their kids and grandchildren. For them this was not just one out of many activities, but instead was an important and integrated part of their lives.

To run a campaign for years costs money. Even if all work was done on a voluntary basis, some financial resources were needed to run the campaign. A membership fee was combined with donations, lotteries and a market during a festival every summer. People donated local food specialities, cakes, sandwiches and different kinds of merchandise. Cash donations provided a sufficient income for paying the bills.

In interviews, activists expressed their intention to continue until the authorities promised in writing to cancel the plans for waste storage in Kynnefjäll. It was obvious that those politicians and elitists who were in favour of building the storage found these voices naive and a little amusing. But the campaign continued. Every summer there was a new festival, march or a huge public meeting. The vigil became a part of people's regular routine. Many signed up for a shift every two weeks or once a month. Others did so more irregularly. The annual meetings become a routine as well. Media of different kinds joined the routine to cover anniversaries of the vigil. Five and ten year anniversaries received extra attention.

The most frequent question was: How long can you stay here? The interviewees replied with a variant of "forever." The average age of the core activists grew over the years. It was not unusual that the annual meeting had a minute of silence to remember someone who had passed away since the previous meeting.

Another thing with these meetings was the unique relations the campaign developed with the local police. On some of the annual meetings the police choir entertained everyone with songs. They were in total agreement with most other local people that these plans should be stopped. Asked what they would do if called on duty to remove activists trying to prevent the construction, many said "I would call in sick." That was additional proof of the massive support this campaign had in the local communities around the mountain.

This is not the place to tell the full story of this campaign and the stubborn people who ran it. In the end, the letter they had been waiting for arrived. In February 2000 celebrations could start. All plans for storing nuclear waste in Kynnefjäll were cancelled and the vigil could end. It took almost 19 years and 10 months with a 24-7 vigil and a lot of supporting annual events to gain victory. This was one of the world's longest environmental vigils. It was completely nonviolent and run by ordinary local people who cared about their kids' future.

This campaign can obviously be seen as defence of both the local community, democracy and nature in the region. Some of the lessons to be learned from this case are about what it takes to build a strong and sustainable campaign. The key was to have local people in charge and to search for people who were not too young to be involved in key positions. The many supportive organisations set aside topics they knew they would disagree on. The syndicalist trade union SAC could work with relatively conservative farmer organisations. The Swedish church managed to cooperate with outspoken atheists, and radical environmentalists could join the ranks of traditional centrist political parties. The unifying force for all was the strong wish and commitment to stop the plans to build a nuclear waste storage at Kynnefjäll.

Even if some planning for emergencies took place it was more in the form of discussions than actual practical exercises. Testing of "telephone chains" to gather a substantial number of people in a short time was done and some civil disobedience training took place during the summer camps organised by the campaigns. It was also a resource that many of the activists who took their 12-hour turns in the cabin were experienced people who had been part of large-scale nonviolent actions in other struggles.

Assessment

We can assess the Kynnefjäll campaign in terms of how it contributes to promoting social defence, in particular to developing the capacity to resist aggression and repression as an alternative to the military. To do this, we look at five areas: awareness, valuing, understanding, endorsement and action.

Awareness: Does the campaign help make people more aware of social defence? The Kynnefjäll campaign made participants aware of how nonviolent action can be used to resist government plans potentially backed by force. In this aspect, it definitely made people more aware of the capacity to resist repression. On the other hand, it was not connected to awareness of nonviolent action as a systematic alternative to military defence.

Valuing: Does the campaign help make people value social defence? The Kynnefjäll campaign made participants value nonviolent action against the government. On the other hand, it was not connected to valuing nonviolent action as a systematic alternative to military defence.

Understanding: Does the campaign help people understand social defence?

The Kynnefjäll campaign helped participants better understand the methods and dynamics of nonviolent action. On the other hand, it was not linked to understanding of nonviolent action as a systematic alternative to military defence.

Endorsement: *Does the campaign lead respected groups to endorse social defence?*
The Kynnefjäll campaign showed the power of sustained nonviolent action, and thus promoted greater respect for activists and their methods. It built respect and solidarity between diverse constituencies. However, it did not lead any prestigious groups to endorse social defence or even nonviolent action.

Action: *Does the campaign give participants greater experience in social defence activities?*
For participants, the Kynnefjäll campaign provided a powerful learning experience in how to use nonviolent action for a valued cause. It thus laid the basis for applying the same skills and insights to defending nonviolently against aggression and repression in other circumstances.

In summary, the Kynnefjäll campaign provided experiences that would help in a system of social defence, but did not directly contribute to bringing about a social defence system. This conclusion would apply to many other nonviolent campaigns: they contribute to awareness, valuing and understanding of nonviolent action, but without a direct connection to promoting social defence.

These same five criteria – awareness, valuing, understanding, endorsement and action – can be applied to other activities, as a way of assessing whether they contribute to the longer term goal of building a social defence system.

9
Questions and responses

What's the difference between nonviolent action and social defence?

Social defence is an application of nonviolent action for a particular purpose: to defend a community against aggression and repression. Nonviolent action can also be used for other purposes, for example for promoting social change, defending conditions of employment, protesting at an injustice, and intervening between opposing armed forces.

Some people look at things a bit differently. Nonviolence can be thought of as a way of life that involves adopting suitable personal values and engaging in constructive actions to build a cooperative, self-reliant society. This conception of nonviolence involves more than methods of social and political action. In some ways this conception is closer to social defence.

Some people think of social defence as any action that resists domination by powerful groups, notably the military, the government and large corporations. This conception of social defence is closer to nonviolent action as a method of social and political action.

We think it's important to think of social defence as an alternative to military methods. But it's useful to remember that not everyone uses terms the same way.

How can people be recruited to participate in social defence?

There is no single answer to how to recruit members and activists to contribute to a social defence system. As for most civil society organisations, a lot will be based on voluntary participation. For some functions, we can imagine having people working in a more professional capacity and receiving a salary. Greenpeace, for example, in its campaigns relies on a core group of paid staff combined with volunteers. A social defence network might use a similar combination. Some of the skills needed for an efficient social defence may require doing it as a profession with regular time for exercises and skills development. A system of obligatory conscription is not a good idea. The level of commitment, creativity, courage and personal sacrifice needed requires personal commitment that is unlikely to be present when people are forced to join or do it only for the money.

What about ruthless enemies?

There are no guarantees for the outcomes of any conflicts. Interactions with ruthless actors are very complex and there are many groups involved, in other words many stakeholders. Most presentations of such conflicts in the media and academia are extremely simplified. There are good reasons for making some simplifications; an obvious one is that an accurate description would be almost impossible to understand and huge when it comes to words and pictures. It is too complex for any single observer to have a complete overview. There will always be a need to make a selection of what to focus on.

The main problem when it comes to cases like the genocide in Rwanda 1994, Indonesian massacre of people accused of being communists in 1965–1966, the massacre of civilians in Hiroshima and Nagasaki in August 1945, the Holocaust in Ukraine 1941–1944, the Japanese killing in Nanjing 1937–1938 or the massacre of Armenians 1894–1896 is that the simplifications and analysis are so gross that it is almost impossible to imagine any outcome other than what in fact happened. The few stakeholders mentioned are described as completely homogeneous and monolithic with no nuances.

Many of the presentations create the impression that the process is like a natural law with only one achievable result.

In large scale societal conflicts where some of the stakeholders have used massive violence it takes some more advanced analytical skills to see that the black and white picture in fact is filled with many colours.

There is not a single historical case where every person involved functioned like a cog in well-oiled machinery. Part of a social defence strategy can be to encourage and help adversaries to behave less violently, to desert or even act against their own commanders.

To actively search for individuals or units that might be willing to change sides is a strategy with a potential to reduce atrocities of many kinds. The many stories from Rwanda in 1994 of Hutus helping victims from the Tutsi community shows us that this is not happening by coincidence. Despite massive propaganda to justify brutal violence against a stigmatised group some stood against the pressure to act in accordance with the dominant discourse.

Similar stories are well known from the Nazi regime in Germany.[125] During WWII, prisoners of war from Yugoslavia who worked in German arms factories made some of the bombs useless and hence saved many lives when they did not explode as expected. Seamen on ships and boats from Norway on their way to UK during the war reported that many of the German bombs dropped like stones in the sea without exploding. Years after the war the story behind these sabotaged bombs was published. If such stories were well known and discussed as part of a strategy for social defence we could expect more lives to be saved.

In a context where social defence is the norm, ideas for resistance will be a part of everyday thinking. Complete obedience to commit gross human rights violations will be difficult to imagine.

---

125 Majken Jul Sørensen, "Glorifications and simplifications in case studies of Danish WWII nonviolent resistance," *Journal of Resistance Studies*, vol. 3, no. 1, 2017, pp. 99–137; Nathan Stoltzfus, *Resistance of the Heart: Intermarriage and the Rosenstrasse Protest in Nazi Germany* (New York: Norton, 1996); Nechama Tec, *Resistance: Jews and Christians Who Defied the Nazi Terror* (Oxford: Oxford University Press, 2013).

What about defending against genocide?

Genocide is mass killing of civilians.[126] How can social defence possibly resist it?

It's useful to look at different contexts for genocide in recent history. Some genocides are undertaken by repressive governments against segments of their own people. Examples are the Soviet Union under Stalin and China under Mao Tse Tung. Social defence is designed for resisting repression, and in a social defence system there is no military, so this sort of genocide would not be possible.

Closely related are cases in which militaries were unleashed against part of the population, for example Indonesia in 1965–1966 and Bangladesh in 1971 when it became independent of Pakistan. Social defence is suited for defending against such attacks. It is important to note that the existence of military forces enables such genocides. In other words, the military is the source of the danger and social defence is a road for countering or removing the source.

Genocide is almost always linked to war.[127] The mobilisation of the army and the population against an external enemy is channelled against a portion of the domestic population that is treated as if it is the enemy. The Holocaust under the Nazis only began after the German invasion of the Soviet Union. The genocide of the Armenians by the Turkish government occurred during World War I. The genocide in Rwanda in 1994 occurred while the government was fighting the Rwandan Patriotic Front based in Uganda.

---

126 The United Nations Genocide Convention defines genocide in a particular way that excludes certain types of mass killing (such as for political reasons) and includes some actions without direct killing. We follow here the usage of many scholars in using "genocide" to refer to any large, systematic killing of civilians. See Adam Jones, *Genocide: A Comprehensive Introduction* (London: Routledge, 2006), pp. 8–28.

127 Martin Shaw, *War and Genocide: Organized Killing in Modern Society* (Cambridge: Polity, 2003).

As noted, social defence prepares the population to resist aggression and repression, so it far better suited to oppose mass killing led by governments and militaries, which are the source of the danger. With a social defence system, there would be no military forces and therefore no organised basis for waging violent warfare. It is implausible to imagine a population committed to nonviolence engaging in genocide.

Although militaries are the main agent for genocidal killing, there can still be a fear that replacing the military by civilian resistance makes a population vulnerable to mass killing by some foreign military. The best examples of this are in the history of imperialism, when the militaries from Spain, Portugal, Belgium, Britain, Netherlands, France and Germany conquered populations in the Americas, Africa, Asia and Australasia. In quite a few of these areas, massive numbers of indigenous people were killed, starved or enslaved.

The initial conquest of the Americas by Spanish and Portuguese invaders was long before several important developments: a sensibility about human rights, the rise of numerous independent activist groups, and modern communication methods. In the past century, nearly every major genocide has taken place in secret, with perpetrators seeking to hide their actions from the wider world. Mass killing in China and the Soviet Union was hidden from people outside. The mass starvation during China's "Great Leap Forward" in the late 1950s is even now a taboo topic in China and little known elsewhere. The Holocaust was carried out in secret. Although many people in Nazi Germany knew about the killings, there was no announcement by the government that Jews and others were being murdered. Quite the contrary: many efforts were made to keep knowledge of the operation on a need-to-know basis.

With a social defence system, defenders would be prepared to record, document and expose any killings. They would also be prepared to counter the other methods used by genocide perpetrators to reduce public outrage: devaluing the target; reinterpreting the actions by lying, minimising consequences, blaming others and benevolent framing; using official channels to give an appearance of justice; and intimidating opponents and rewarding supporters.[128]

---

128 On these tactics, see Brian Martin, "Managing outrage over genocide: case study Rwanda," *Global Change, Peace & Security,* vol. 21, no. 3, 2009, pp. 275–290.

Today there are dozens of small countries without armies and therefore unable to defend against an aggressor that wanted nothing more than killing all the population. Why have there been no mass killings in any of these countries? Imagine an aggressor that decided to invade Costa Rica, which has no army, just to kill everyone. It is totally implausible today, and even more implausible if Costa Ricans were prepared to expose the attack to the wider world.

Perhaps fear that disarmament would expose a population to fearsome killers is based on illusions that persist despite lack of evidence or logic.

Defending against military invasions might have been relevant years ago, but today the possibility of invasion and conquest of any large country is minimal. Therefore, defence against foreign aggression is not a good rationale for social defence.

It is true that using armies to conquer entire countries seems less common than in times gone by. Alexander the Great was known for his conquests in Europe and Asia. Imperialism involved conquering and occupying vast areas of the planet. During World War II, Nazi Germany conquered much of Europe.

Since then, there are fewer examples of wars used to invade and occupy foreign lands. It's possible to think of the Russian conquest of the Crimea, the 2001 invasion of Afghanistan and the 2003 invasion of Iraq, and quite a number of others. But an invasion of any major country seems off the agenda.

So why would social defence need to be concerned about foreign aggressors? A primary reason is that people believe in the ideology of defence. In Australia, many people believe military defence is essential because otherwise the country is vulnerable to foreign aggressors.

In many countries, there is no serious external threat. The main function of social defence therefore is to oppose repression by the government. In Fiji, for example, there is no threat from foreign invaders. The principal role of the Fiji military has been to take over the government and oppress the population.

Social defence can't defend remote territories.

True enough. If the Russian military invaded the remote north of Sweden, where few people live, then the local possibilities of resistance are limited. If some foreign military invaded Christmas Island, a remote Australian territory in the Indian Ocean, local possibilities for resistance would be limited.

The issue of remote territories points to a key difference between military defence and social defence. Military defence is usually seen as defence of the territory administered by a state, whereas social defence is defence of what people consider important, such as freedom, equality and community.

The issue of territory shows that social defence is not a functional replacement for military defence. In other words, it doesn't replace all the functions of military defence. On the other hand, it accomplishes things a military cannot, such as fostering the capacity of a population to act together in defence of basic values that do not involve physical force or killing.

Setting these issues aside, consider what a society could do about an invasion and occupation of remote territories. Although local resistance would be limited due to lack of population, resistance is still possible by publicising the attack, seeking support from the population of the aggressor force, organising boycotts, protesting at international events, and a host of other actions. The impact of these actions would depend on the perceived justice of the cause of the defenders and on the connections that social defenders had built up around the globe.

In a social defence system, is there any role for military forces?

It depends on what you call military forces. Undoubtedly there will continue to be roles that involve courage and skills to tackle physical challenges. Gene Keyes in a 1982 article titled "Force without firepower" describes a wide range of roles for "troops" without weapons.[129] He calls this unarmed military service, though a different name might be better, given that many

---

129 Gene Keyes, "Force without firepower: a doctrine of unarmed military service," *CoEvolution Quarterly*, Summer 1982, pp. 4–25. A 2014 version of this article is titled "To Give Life: A Nonkilling Military. Precedents and Possibilities", www.genekeyes.com/To-Give-Life.html.

people think "military forces" are bound to be armed.

In peacetime, he describes three roles. The first is rescue, such as when miners are trapped underground or people are swept away in a flood. Rescues today are carried out by special emergency services, or sometimes by police or military forces. Weapons are seldom needed, but bravery and skills are definitely necessary.

A second peacetime role is civic action, which refers to contributing to social services such as construction, farming, education and other community development projects. Militaries sometimes engage in such projects. They do not require arms.

A third peacetime role is what Keyes calls "colossal action." This involves enormous enterprises such as planting giant tree belts to halt erosion, building a large-scale renewable energy system, and building sea walls to hold back tides.

Keyes says that in a world without armaments, or where communities are disarming, there actually may be more conflict, and a need to wage conflicts without violence. He tells of four conflict roles for unarmed services. One is "friendly persuasion," which includes everything from face-to-face conversations to air drops of leaflets. It can also involve providing food and consumer goods. Imagine, instead of dropping bombs, aeroplanes dropping packages of basic supplies and luxuries, intended to win over rather than destroy opponent troops and civilians.

Three other conflict roles are guerrilla action, police action, and buffer action, all unarmed. These correspond to well-established modes of nonviolent action. "Buffer action" involves civilians placing themselves between warring groups to deter them from fighting.[130] This requires great courage.

Finally, there are roles for unarmed services in classic war scenarios. One is defence, which includes frontline social defence roles in protests, strikes and bodily interventions. Another is expeditionary action: a team of unarmed activists would set out to intervene against armed forces at a distant location. Finally there is invasion, in which the invaders are unarmed, to oppose mass violence or severe oppression.

---

130 Yeshua Moser-Puangsuwan and Thomas Weber (eds.), *Nonviolent Intervention across Borders: A Recurrent Vision* (Honolulu, HI: Spark M. Matsunaga Institute for Peace, University of Hawai'i, 2000).

Keyes' message is that there are many roles for unarmed soldiers, roles involving courage, skills and the willingness to risk their lives, in other words to do everything that armed soldiers do, and more, except for killing others.

What about an invasion in which no one is killed?

In most discussions of social defence, the assumption is that invaders will use force, or the threat of force, to subdue the population. But there are other

scenarios of takeover that do not involve physical violence.[131] If aggressors avoid using violence, they also avoid generating the outrage and hostility that violence often fosters.

A well-prepared resistance would involve rallies, fraternisation, strikes, boycotts, blockades and many other techniques. Rather than use force, the invaders might instead ignore rallies and other protests, argue with resisters who engage with them, wait for strikes and boycotts to fizzle out, and avoid confronting blockades. The invaders would use patience rather than force,

---

131 Frank Deroose, "Need military aggressors kill people?" *Interdisciplinary Peace Research*, vol. 1, no. 2, 1990, pp. 27–37.

gradually infiltrate themselves into the society and seek to promote their ways of thinking and behaving, hoping for the resistance to die down. The invaders might be armed, but by not using their weapons they might actually achieve more.

This is a possible scenario, but it is not such a frightening one. It becomes a struggle between opponents that each refrain from using violence. If this is a future for invasions, then why bother with arms at all?

Isn't social defence conservative, because it involves defence of the status quo? Is there capacity for bringing about social change?

Social defence is indeed defence of the status quo because it is *defence* of society against aggression or repression. This is actually one of its great strengths. In a society, it can be hard to bring about change. Many people are committed to existing beliefs and practices. This is why feminists, environmentalists and other campaigners have taken such a long time to bring about change.

Nonviolent action is normally seen as a tool for social change, for example to resist a repressive government or to challenge racial discrimination. It is often very hard to get people to participate.

Thinking of nonviolent action for defence changes things considerably. People will defend what they have much more readily. They just need to have the skills and understanding for doing it effectively.

10

Conclusion

The contemporary military system is enormously powerful, in several ways. There are millions of trained soldiers and vast quantities of weapons, along with the infrastructure to build and support the system, from teachers and scientists to cooks and accountants. It seems fanciful to imagine replacing this system with a different system, one that does not involve violence.

Perhaps the greatest strength of the military system is its hold over people's minds. Governments and the media promote the belief that "defence" means military preparedness or even military interventions, and that there is no other effective way to provide security. Past soldiers and wars are glorified. Many people are so highly committed to military thinking that any alternative is seen as a threat.

It is useful to remember that today's military systems are quite new in terms of human evolution. Agriculture, which makes possible the accumulation of a sizeable economic surplus that can support a military class, is only ten thousand or so years old. Nation states and their mass armies are only a few hundred years old. Advanced weapons, such as machine guns and missiles, are even newer. What seems natural and inevitable today would have been unbelievable to someone living a thousand years ago.

Along with the rise of military systems there was the rise in a different vision, a vision of a world without violence. This has been persistently present, and has inspired peace movements for centuries. However, there is no single picture of a world without war and a world with social justice. One picture is of a world without conflict, in which everyone lives in harmony. Another is of a world government, which maintains peace through a monopoly over arms.

In this book, we have presented a different picture, of a world in which there is quite a bit of conflict, and in which conflict is resolved without violence. This vision is inspired by the successes of nonviolent action – rallies, strikes, boycotts, sit-ins and other methods of protest, noncooperation and intervention – in major struggles. Nonviolent campaigns have been effective in resisting repressive governments and in challenging oppressive systems such as slavery. Social movements today, including the labour, feminist and

157

environmental movements, rely primarily on either conventional political action or nonviolent action. Armed struggle is increasingly rejected as a road to social emancipation.

Despite the successes of nonviolent campaigns, military systems seem little affected. The era of mass conscript armies is in decline, being replaced by voluntary armies supported by advanced weaponry. The next stage in war-fighting will involve automated weapons. Drones, remotely piloted, are already well established. In the future, more weapons systems will operate using artificial intelligence, providing new challenges for opponents of war. As well, this suggests that military systems are not likely to fade away soon.

In this context, in which militaries seem so highly entrenched, part of the material and mental landscape, social defence can seem utopian, as an unachievable goal. But it is not so long ago that women's emancipation seemed utopian.

Although social defence may not become a reality for many decades, it can serve as a guide for action, in a host of domains. Social defence involves increasing the capacity of ordinary people to resist external aggression, and this necessarily means increasing the capacity to resist their own government. Hence social defence provides a guide for community empowerment that can challenge many different types of domination: by governments, employers, bureaucratic systems and economic systems, national and international. In its deepest formulation, social defence implies the restructuring of social institutions to empower populations.

In trying to move towards social defence, today we can see only some of the challenges ahead. If successful steps forward are made, no doubt new obstacles will become apparent and new insights and methods will be needed to address them.

Further reading

Links to many of the articles and books cited in the text, and the short pieces below, are available at http://www.bmartin.cc/pubs/19sd/.

Short surveys of ideas about social defence

Phil Bogdonoff, "CBD: a short history," *Civilian Based Defense: News & Opinion,* November 1982, pp. 3–5

Christopher Kruegler, "Civilian-based defense: the intellectual antecedents," *Civilian Based Defense: News & Opinion,* vol. 4, no. 3, March 1988, pp. 1–4

Short critical assessments of social defence

Hajo Karbach, "The myths of alternative defence," *WRI Open Forum,* from *Graswurzelrevolution,* Summer 1981

Wolfgang Sternstein, "Strategies of transition to social defense," *Civilian Based Defense: News & Opinion,* vol. 6, no. 1, July/August 1989, pp. 8–10

Selected works of significance

American Friends Service Committee (James Bristol et al.), *In Place of War: An Inquiry into Nonviolent National Defense* (New York: Grossman, 1967)
This is a systematic treatment covering preparation and training, historical examples, organisation and strategy for the resistance, foreign policy considerations, and ways to promote nonviolent defence. Many relevant issues are addressed, including noncooperation with invaders, sabotage (not recommended), personal contact with invaders and influencing the invader's population. Ideas are presented for action by churches, universities, unions, the peace movement and other groups. As the title indicates, the focus is on national defence against foreign invaders.

Anders Boserup and Andrew Mack, *War Without Weapons: Non-violence in National Defence* (London: Frances Pinter, 1974)
Boserup and Mack analyse studies of nonviolent defence from a critical though sympathetic perspective, discussing positive and negative modes of

defence, methods of civilian defence, organisational problems (including the role of leadership), an analogy with guerrilla warfare, dealing with repression, case studies (Ruhr, Czechoslovakia, etc.), and problems in combining civilian and military defence. Chapter 10 looks at nonviolent defence in the light of classical strategic theory, arguing that the centre of gravity of a nonviolent defence system – the most important thing to be defended – is the unity of the resistance.

Bulletin of Peace Proposals, vol. 9, no. 4, 1978
This issue contains a number of informed academic assessments of social defence. Authors include Johan Galtung, Gustaaf Geeraerts, Adam Roberts and Gene Sharp.

Robert J. Burrowes, *The Strategy of Nonviolent Defense: A Gandhian Approach* (Albany, NY: State University of New York Press, 1996)
Burrowes begins with a critique of classical ideas about strategy and concludes with several chapters laying out the strategy of nonviolent defence. The central message of the book is encapsulated in a table on page 209 stating that the political purpose of nonviolent defence is "to create the policy, process, structural, and systemic conditions that will satisfy human needs." Within this general framework, there are two strategic aims, one for the defence and one for the counteroffensive. For the defence, the strategic aim is "to consolidate the power and will of the defending population to resist the aggression." This includes mobilisation of "key social groups" including worker organisations, women's groups, religious bodies and ethnic communities. Parallel to the strategic aim of the defence is the strategic aim of the counteroffensive: "to *alter* the will of the opponent elite to conduct the aggression, and to *undermine* their power to do so."
Burrowes traces the implications of his general framework through a range of areas, including the time frame of the struggle, communication with the opponent, selection of nonviolent tactics, secrecy, sabotage, maintaining nonviolent discipline and making defenders less vulnerable in the face of an extremely ruthless opponent.

Howard Clark, "Nonviolent resistance and social defence," in Gail Chester and Andrew Rigby (eds.), *Articles of Peace: Celebrating Fifty Years of Peace News* (Bridport, Dorset: Prism, 1986), pp. 49–69
Clark was closely involved with the peace movement. He provides a

valuable assessment of pacifist views (via coverage in the magazine *Peace News*), nonviolent action and social defence, seeing social defence as action today against domination. He surveys views about social defence – Gene Sharp, Adam Roberts, Bob Overy and others – in the context of changing conditions, including anti-racism and the movement against nuclear power.

Giliam de Valk in cooperation with Johan Niezing, *Research on Civilian-Based Defence* (Amsterdam: SISWO, 1993)
This short book describes 24 topics for research into civilian-based defence, for example addressing repression technologies, instructions to civil servants, the history of nonviolent struggle, the centre of gravity and the role of intelligence services. The ideas for the research proposals grew out of a Dutch government committee that investigated social defence, a subsequent study group, and de Valk's own additions. The proposals are valuable in themselves and are an inspiration to think of what needs to be learned about civilian-based defence.

Antonino Drago, *Difesa Popolare Nonviolenta: Premesse Teoriche, Principi Politici e Nuovi Scenari [Nonviolent Popular Defense: Theoretical Premises, Political Principles and New Scenarios]* (Turin: EGA, 2006)
The establishment of voluntary civil service and the suspension of compulsory military service show that the debate on alternative solutions to conflicts continues to make important progress. Drago's work on nonviolent popular defense and on alternative solutions to conflicts is a text for all scholars of popular diplomacy, peacekeeping, peaceful conflict management and, more generally, issues related to so-called "science for peace." [adapted from Amazon.it]

Theodor Ebert, *Soziale Verteidigung. Band 1, Historische Erfahrungen und Grundzüge der Strategie; Band 2: Formen und Bedingungen des Zivilen Widerstandes* (Waldkirch: Waldkircher Verlag, 1981)
Ebert has researched important examples of earlier nonviolent resistance, e.g. the 1953 East German uprising, and has been a leading theorist of nonviolent action and civilian defence since the 1960s. Both volumes of *Soziale Verteidigung* are compilations of articles Ebert wrote on the subject in the 1970s. Volume 1: Historical Experience and Fundamentals of Strategy; Volume 2: Forms and Conditions of the Civil Resistance.

J. P. Feddema, A. H. Heering and E. A. Huisman, *Verdediging met een menselijk gezicht: grondslagen en praktijk van sociale verdediging [Defense with a human face: foundations and practice of social defence]* (Amersfoort, Netherlands: De Horstink, 1982)

Although much is said and written about nuclear weapons, the following two key questions are rarely discussed: Is the idea that a people should be able to defend themselves with military force still acceptable? Can not the safety of our society be better defended by other means? The authors of this book want to fill this gap. They point to the principled and practical arguments that argue for social rather than military defence. By this they mean a system to protect democracy and its development by means of nonviolent methods and techniques that are compatible with the basic values of democracy. The nature of these methods and techniques and the way in which the switchover to the new system can take place are discussed extensively. [from the book jacket]

Johan Galtung, *Forsvar uten militærvesen: et pasifistisk grunnsyn [Defence without a military system: a Pacifist Worldview]* ([Oslo]: Folkereisning mot krig, 1958)

In this very early book Galtung presents how a national defence could be established and function based on the principles of pacifism. This book brings the ideas of Gandhi into a new arena: a modern liberal welfare state and the need to establish a system for the defence of such a state. It initiated a whole new way of thinking for the newly established academic field of peace research as well as for a growing peace movement.

Johan Galtung, *Peace, War and Defense. Essays in Peace Research, Volume Two* (Copenhagen: Christian Ejlers, 1976)

War, Peace and Defense is a collection of insightful and stimulating essays oriented towards classifying and probing seldom investigated concepts and areas. Much of the writing is abstract. "Two concepts of defense" (pp. 328–340) compares territorial and social defence and lists ten sources of guerrilla success and the implications for nonmilitary defence. "On the strategy of nonmilitary defense. Some proposals and problems" (pp. 378–426) examines strategies aimed at the antagonist (such as noncooperation), strategies aimed at self-protection (such as self-reliance in communication and transport), and strategies aimed at deterring the antagonist (including training in methods of nonviolent action).

Gustaaf Geeraerts (editor), *Possibilities of Civilian Defence in Western Europe* (Amsterdam: Swets and Zeitlinger, 1977)
Leading researchers look at civilian defence, providing a variety of perspectives. Especially useful are discussions of the political implications of civilian defence, the conditions for its expansion, links to socialism and to European states, the role of peace research, and grassroots versus top-down initiatives.

Berit G. Holm, *Teknisk moralisme: i teori for ikkevoldsaksjon og "civilian defence." Kritisk analyse av Gene Sharp's ikkevoldsteori [Technical moralism: in theory of nonviolence action and "civilian defense." Critical Analysis of Gene Sharp's Nonviolence Theory.]* (Oslo: Institutt for Filosofi, 1978)
Berit Holm present arguments against Gene Sharp and his theories for nonviolent action and civilian-based defence. Her main critique is lack of morality in his concepts and too much focus on techniques.

Evert A. Huisman, *Van geweld bevrijd: overleven door democratisering en ontwapening [Freed from Violence: Surviving by Democratizing and Disarmament]* (Zwolle, Netherlands: Stichting Voorlichting Aktieve Geweldloosheid, 1987)
Huisman surveys threats facing societies, discusses the functions usually attributed to the military complex and looks at the sorts of alternatives people are searching for. He then addresses nonviolent defence, in particular how it can function, and looks at how to promote participatory democracy.

Jørgen Johansen, *Aldri mer 9. april: sivilmotstand i Halden kommune. En skisse til planlegging [Never More April 9th: Social Defence in the municipality of Halden. A Sketch for planning]* (Oslo: Folkereisning mot krig, 1988)
This is a detailed plan for how to defend the Norwegian city of Halden. Plans for civil society actors, business communities and authorities are presented. It is a practically oriented book with ideas for what the different actors and sectors in a municipality could do in case of a military invasion.

Jørgen Johansen, *Socialt Försvar: En Ickevåldsrevolution [Social Defence: A nonviolent Revolution]* (NU: Morjärv, 1990)
This is a book written for the Green Party in Sweden when they wanted to develop their party policy on issues like defence and security. It describes a social defence for the people and social institutions rather than territory. It emphasises the need for a completely new way of thinking.

Jørgen Johansen, *Sosialt forsvar: ikkevoldskamp mot vår tids trusler [Social Defence: Nonviolent Struggle against the Threats of Our Time]* (Oslo: Militærnekterforl, 2000).

This book present theories and plans for defending a state like Norway against the threats against democracy, nature, freedom, and human rights. With examples from civil society and WWII, the text gives an overview of the possibilities for building a defence system. Ideas from Gene Sharp are put in a Norwegian context and developed further.

Gene Keyes, "Strategic non-violent defense: the construct of an option," *Journal of Strategic Studies,* vol. 4, no. 2, June 1981, pp. 125–151

Drawing on his study of Danish resistance to the Nazis, Keyes argues that the purpose of social defence is not survival but defence of principles. He says the centre of gravity of the defence is the morale of the resistance.

Gene Keyes, "Heavy casualties and nonviolent defense," *Philosophy and Social Action,* vol. 17, nos. 3–4, July-December 1991, pp. 75–88.

Keyes says nonviolent defence planning should include worst-case scenarios, such as being prepared for brutality, torture, mass killing and nuclear extortion. These possibilities are seldom addressed in writings on nonviolent defence.

Stephen King-Hall, *Defence in the Nuclear Age* (London: Victor Gollancz, 1958)

King-Hall was in the British navy 1914–1929. After retirement he became an author and commentator, and served as an independent member of parliament 1939–1944. In this book, King-Hall says the overwhelming threat posed by nuclear weapons means there is a need for a nonviolent approach. *Defence in the Nuclear Age* is one of the first detailed accounts of how a social defence system might operate. King-Hall says the basis of war is political, not military, and that what should be defended is not territory but a way of life. He was anti-communist and believed in the value of current British parliamentary democracy, but his ideas can be applied to other sorts of societies and threats.

Herbert M. Kritzer, "Nonviolent national defense: concepts and implications," *Peace Research Reviews,* vol. 5, April 1974, pp. 1–57

Kritzer surveys ideas and writings about nonviolent defence, covering numerous early publications. He also examines two recent case studies and provides an extensive bibliography.

Bradford Lyttle, *National Defense Thru Nonviolent Resistance* (Chicago, IL: Shahn-ti Sena, 1958)
In this short book, Lyttle aruges that nonviolent defence is needed and possible, while saying relatively little about the methods of nonviolent action. He refers throughout to Christian ideals but makes his case mostly in pragmatic terms. Lyttle presents a programme of conversion to nonviolent defence led by the US government, with the agreement of Congress, over a period of three years, thus revealing a naïve faith in the power of ideas to deal with entrenched militarism.

Brian Martin, *Social Defence, Social Change* (London: Freedom Press, 1993)
Social defence is presented as a key feature of a grassroots strategy to challenge and replace the war system. Included are discussions of feminism, the police, the environment, telecommunications, and implications for political and economic systems.

Brian Martin, *Technology for Nonviolent Struggle* (London: War Resisters' International, 2001)
Research and development relevant to a number of areas, especially communication and survival, are assessed for their relevance to nonviolent struggle. Reorienting technology from military to nonviolence goals leads to a recasting of research methods and priorities.

Christian Mellon, Jean Marie Muller and Jacques Sémelin, *La dissuasion civile: principes et méthodes de la résistance non violente dans la stratégie française [Civil deterrence: principles and methods of nonviolent resistance in the French strategy]* (Paris: Fondation pour les études de défense nationale, 1985)
In this work the idea of nonviolent defence is discussed in a French context. The main emphasis is on how a well-developed defence based on nonviolent principles would function as a deterrent for any enemy who might look into the possibility of attacking France.

Motståndsutredningen, *Kompletterande motståndsformer: betänkande [Forms of Complementary Resistance: A Report]* (Stockholm: Liber/Allmänna förl, 1984)
This is a governmental report of how to add a nonviolent element to military defence. It suggests methods, organisational structures, roles for religious

communities and other parts of civil society. An appendix, larger than the actual report, was written by Lennart Bergfeldt. This appendix describes how a Swedish nonviolent national defence could look like. The report was seen as a huge step in the direction of recognising nonviolent defence as a component of the national defence, and a commission was established. Some years later these ideas were dead in the Swedish discussion.

Barbara Müller, *Passiver Widerstand im Ruhrkampf: eine Fallstudie zur gewaltlosen zwischenstaatlichen Konfliktaustragung und ihren Erfolgsbedingungen [Passive Resistance in the Ruhr Struggle: a case study of interstate conflict resolution and its conditions of Success]* (Münster, Germany: Lit, 1995)

Barbara Müller presents a comprehensive and in-depth study of the use on nonviolent defence strategies and techniques during the French occupation of the Ruhr region of Germany between January 1923 and August 1925. This is one of the classical examples of social defence in European history.

Johan Niezing, *Sociale Verdediging als Logisch Alternatief: van Utopie naar Optie [Social Defense as Logical Alternative: from Utopia to Option]* (Assen/Maastricht, Netherlands: Van Gorcum, 1987)

Nuclear weapons, conventional weapons and chemical weapons are inhuman deterrents that threaten to destroy humanity. Social defence is a human and therefore logical alternative as a deterrent. Niezing shows how social defence becomes a deterrent and therefore a defensive means. It requires a broad basis in society. Niezing offers a useful model for introducing social defence that appeals to everyone, both professionals and citizens. [text adapted from the book cover]

Ulf Norenius, *Att vägra leva på knä [To Refuse Living on Your Knees]* (Göteborg, Sweden: Haga i samarbete med SAC's antimilitaristiska komm, 1983)

This book was published by the Anti-militaristic Committee of the Syndicalist Trade Union. Norenius describes a system for social defence that reduces the role of the state. Trade unions and other parts of civil society play a central role in making the society impossible to rule and control by foreign powers as well as by authoritarian and undemocratic domestic rulers. Massive civil disobedience, sabotage, and construction of alternative societies are important ingredients.

Ulf Norenius, *Alternativ beredskap: SAC i kris- och krigstider [Alternative Emergency Response, SAC in Times of Crisis and Emergencies]* (Göteborg, Sweden: Haga, 1986)
In this book Norenius specifically analyses what the trade union SAC should do in crises and emergencies. The union's national network with local groups in industries, transportation companies and other kinds of production could play a vital role in both preventing occupiers access to these services and making sure the local population get what they need.

Michael Randle, *Civil Resistance* (London: Fontana, 1994)
Randle provides a tour through ideas and examples about civil resistance, otherwise known as nonviolent action, in one of the most readable accounts available. The book includes an extensive discussion of "defence by civil resistance," one of the names for social defence. Randle gives a nice account of the development of the idea of social defence, discusses different views on strategy, and analyses links with democracy, both parliamentary and popular. Randle devotes many pages to discussing government interest in civil resistance (limited though it had been) and to discussing the views of leading theorists, but doesn't discuss grassroots strategies.

Adam Roberts (editor), *The Strategy of Civilian Defence: Non-violent Resistance to Aggression* (London: Faber and Faber, 1967)
This is a valuable collection of treatments by leading researchers, covering forms of military attack, the coup d'état, methods of nonviolent action, cases studies from Germany, Norway and Denmark, lessons from guerrilla movements, and policy for civilian defence.

Adam Roberts, *Civilmotståndets teknik [The Techniques of Civilian Resistance]* (Stockholm: Folk och Försvar, 1976)
This book was published by the leading defence establishment in Sweden at a time when few outside a small circle of academics took any notice of any concepts for defence other than the traditional military options. There was a window of opportunity in the late 1970s and first half of the 1980s, but none in the political establishment took alternative defence options seriously enough. Roberts' contribution was to introduce Gene Sharp and other leading theorists to the Swedish discussion.

Alex P. Schmid, in collaboration with Ellen Berends and Luuk Zonneveld, *Social Defence and Soviet Military Power: An Inquiry into the Relevance of an Alternative Defence Concept* (Leiden: Center for the Study of Social Conflict, State University of Leiden, September 1985)

This book contains a wealth of historical material and analysis, and a carefully argued conclusion. It is perhaps the most significant argument made against social defence.

The book contains four parts. The first is a short survey of concepts of nonviolence and social defence. The second is major study of Soviet military interventions and nuclear threats since 1945, including conflicts within the Soviet bloc, conflicts between the Soviet Union and the West, and Soviet involvement in Third World conflicts. A short section describes implications for social defence.

The third part presents four East European case studies: Lithuanian resistance against the Soviet re-occupation (1944 to about 1952), East Germany 1953, Hungary 1956 and Czechoslovakia 1968. In each case, the events are compared with ten "conditions" for social defence to judge whether social defence would have been more successful than the resistance that actually occurred.

The final part of the book looks at social defence as part of a more comprehensive defence system, examines Sweden's psychological defence, and presents the resource mobilisation perspective (which social scientists use to analyse social movements) as an alternative to the social defence perspective.

Schmid's basic conclusion is that social defence would not work against a Soviet invasion, because the Soviet government is mostly immune to persuasion, publicity and economic pressures. As he puts it, "the Soviet military power instrument cannot be balanced by economic noncooperation and cultural persuasion alone as the USSR is economically invulnerable and culturally impenetrable" (p. 209).

The book's analysis has some weaknesses (http://www.bmartin.cc/pubs/88BRnvt1.html). A few years after it was published, the vulnerability of state socialism to nonviolent resistance was shown by the collapse of Eastern European communist regimes and then the dissolution of the Soviet Union.

Gene Sharp, *Making Europe Unconquerable: The Potential of Civilian-based Deterrence and Defense* (Cambridge, MA: Ballinger, 1985)
Sharp, the leading researcher on nonviolent action, here applies his framework to defending against Soviet aggression and military coups. He provides a rationale for civilian-based defence, gives historical examples, discusses conversion from military to civilian-based defence, and discusses preventing, countering and defeating attacks. The book seems to be written more for a US than a European audience. Sharp assumes civilian-based defence is rational and that governments should be introducing it, and disavows grassroots mobilisation as a strategy for converting to civilian-based defence.

Gene Sharp with the assistance of Bruce Jenkins, *Civilian-Based Defense: A Post-Military Weapons System* (Princeton, NJ: Princeton University Press, 1990)
Sharp argues for civilian-based defence along the same lines as *Making Europe Unconquerable*. He covers historical examples, his theory of power, his framework of the dynamics of nonviolent action, how civilian-based defence would operate, and what governments should do to convert to it.

INDEX

www.ingramcontent.com/pod-product-compliance
Lightning Source LLC
Chambersburg PA
CBHW072248270326
41930CB00010B/2311